ILLUSTRATED ICE HOCKEY RULES

ILLUSTRATED
ICE HOCKEY RULES

Bill Chadwick

Illustrations by George Gorycki

An Associated Features Book

Dolphin Books

Doubleday & Company, Inc.

Garden City, New York   1976

Library of Congress Cataloging in Publication Data

Chadwick, Bill.
Illustrated ice hockey rules.

"An Associated Features book."
"Official NHL rules": p. 119.
1. Hockey—Rules.   2. National Hockey League.
I. National Hockey League. Official rule book.
1976.   II. Title.
GV847.5.C46   796.9′62
ISBN 0-385-11408-7
Library of Congress Catalog Card Number 76–2834

To Millie again

Acknowledgments

Hal Bock of the Associated Press, who was my collaborator on my autobiography, *The Big Whistle*, has been vital to the preparation of the manuscript for *Illustrated Ice Hockey Rules*. He is the most knowledgeable of hockey writers, a total professional in all sports, and I thank him for his contributions here.

Also, my appreciation to the National Hockey League, whose complete rules appear in the Appendixes as a total reference for player, fan, announcer, writer, and official alike.

B.C.

Contents

Introduction

Hockey can trace its origins to the late 1800s, but the game played in those days bore little resemblance to the lightning-fast sport that has evolved from it.

The game began with seven players to a team and upright posts imbedded in the ice to serve as goals. There were no nets, no blue lines, no red lines, and no face-off circles.

By 1911 the game was changed from two 30-minute periods to three 20-minute periods. A year later, 6-man hockey was introduced with the elimination of the rover position—a sort of combination forward-defenseman.

In 1917 the National Hockey League was formed, with 4 teams playing a 22-game schedule. The next year, the schedule was reduced to 18 games. That's a long way from the 18-team, 80-game schedules followed in the NHL today.

In the early days of the NHL there were severe restrictions on forward passing, greatly limiting attack patterns. At the same time, goalies were prohibited from falling to the ice, making defense of their nets a truly difficult proposition.

Those rules were amended in the early 1930s, and shortly after that the penalty shot—perhaps the most exciting one-on-one confrontation in all of sports—was introduced.

During World War II the red line was added to the two blue lines, speeding up the game and signaling the start of what is known as hockey's modern era.

It was about that time that Maurice Richard was emerging as hockey's most explosive scorer—the game's first 50-goal man.

Rapidly, Richard was joined by other enormously talented players, men like Gordie Howe, destined to become the game's all-time highest scorer; Jean Beliveau, one of the game's most skillful skaters, and Bobby Hull, whose slap shot became the most feared offensive weapon in the sport.

Later, there were others—Phil Esposito, the game's first single-season 100-point scorer, and Bobby Orr, a gifted defenseman who became the first player at his position to win a scoring championship.

As the stars proliferated, so did interest in the sport and there was a need for uniform rules and sensible interpretation of them to assure the continued growth of the game.

The NHL Official Rule Book is the bible of hockey regulations. Some leagues will operate with slight alterations, but basically the NHL rules are just about universally accepted as the rules of the sport.

In collegiate hockey, one of the important differences is the existence of an overtime period. The NHL did away with overtimes during World War II, but the NCAA rules call for a 10-minute overtime. The World Hockey Association also used overtimes.

The NCAA also uses two officials for each game, a referee and an assistant referee. Professional hockey, of course, uses a referee and two linesmen.

Another basic difference between college and professional hockey is the absence on the college rink of the center red line that divides the ice in half. That just about eliminates the "two-line pass" offsides infraction.

The same thing is true in international hockey. At one time there were tight checking regulations in both college and international hockey, but both have now altered their rules to the point where checking is about the same as it is in professional hockey.

Another basic difference between collegiate and professional hockey is the requirement that college players wear helmets. Pros are not required to use helmets, although more and more players have adopted this important piece of equipment.

Without rules, hockey would be a formless ballet on ice without rhyme or reason. The rules give the game shape and meaning, a law within which the players must operate and perform.

And the rules don't change the universal, simple basic aim of this game. It still all comes down to shooting the puck into the net—or keeping it out.

ILLUSTRATED ICE HOCKEY RULES

Section 1
THE RINK

There is more to the construction of an ice hockey rink than the simple ice dimensions. The rink is to hockey what the diamond is to baseball, and it's what those 100 yards from end zone to end zone are to football. This is where hockey teams do their thing, and there are definite specifications that must be followed.

The rule books—both professional and collegiate—call for ice surfaces measuring 200 feet long by 85 feet wide, and all new arenas measure those distances. But several of the older rinks are a bit shorter than that 200 feet. Another rule that is not always complied with in the older rinks is the one that says both teams must have their player benches on the same side of the ice, opposite the penalty boxes on the other side of the ice. Two of the exceptions are Boston Garden, home of the Bruins, and the Montreal Forum, where the Canadiens play their games.

Rink doors must be constructed to swing away from the ice area in order to prevent injury to players skating along the sideboards. That wasn't always in the rule book. I can remember specifically that during the 1940s the doors at the Detroit Olympia swung the other way and caused many player injuries.

Detroit had another little wrinkle at the Olympia that provided a major edge for the home team Red Wings until NHL legislation changed it. The Wings had two doors leading from their player bench to the ice, but there was only one door at the visitors' bench. Obviously, that made player changes more difficult for the visiting team, a situation that I can assure you was no accident.

The man responsible for that innovation was Jack Adams, Detroit's long-time general manager, who'd do anything to win a hockey game. Another one of Adams' little tricks was to make sure the Red Wings' bench was much longer than the visitors' bench. That way, Detroit's bench extended far into the end of the ice that the Wings defended for two of the game's three periods. The reasons were obvious, enabling faster changes for his team.

Good coaches can use even something as simple as a players' bench to their advantage. They have their teams seated on the bench in a specific order. The defensemen will be seated at the end of the bench closest to their team's net, so that they can get into position faster. Players on each line will be seated together, so that they can get on the ice as a unit.

So you can see that hockey strategy starts before a team ever gets on the ice.

The Rink

Problem
The officials take the ice five minutes before the scheduled start of play to warm up and examine the nets and ice surface. They may find several irregularities. During the warm-up of the two teams, a hole has been made in one of the nets. There is a spot of ice that is rutted. The ice does not seem to be standard length.

Solution
Before the game starts, the officials are responsible for having all necessary repairs made. The hole in the net is a common problem. All rinks have extra pieces of netting available for some quick mending. The ice ruts can be cured by some water. That's why most rinks keep a gardener's watering can on hand. They sure aren't trying to grow grass out there.

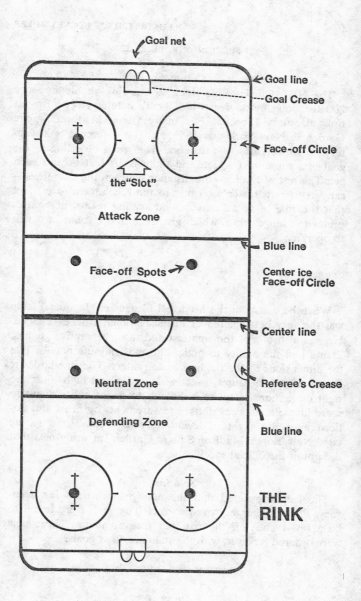

Goal net

Goal line

Goal Crease

Face-off Circle

the "Slot"

Attack Zone

Blue line

Face-off Spots

Center ice
Face-off Circle

Center line

Neutral Zone

Referee's Crease

Defending Zone

Blue line

THE
RINK

SECTION ONE, RULE 2.

Comment

The NHL Official Rule Book says a rink should measure 200 feet long by 85 feet wide. That's a fallacy. The Boston rink measures 186×85. For many years, Madison Square Garden in New York was 185×85. The difference is in center ice. In all rinks, the distance from each blue line to the goal is a standard 60 feet, and there is 10 feet behind each net. The rest of the ice—the distance between the blue lines—can vary from Boston's 46 feet to the recommended 60 feet that the rule book calls for. Good skating teams, of course, prefer the longer rinks which give them more room in which to operate.

The Nets

Problem

When he was with the Montreal Canadiens, Jacques Plante was the very best goaltender in the National Hockey League. He was also one of the smartest and most perceptive goalies. Plante had the ability to notice the most minute details, like the dimensions of the net he had to protect. The standard Art Ross goal net measures 6 feet wide and 4 feet high—just the right dimensions to make it difficult to guard and difficult to score into. Plante knew those measurements by heart and noticed even the slightest deviation from them. For one, he cited New York's Madison Square Garden for using nets that did not fit the official specifications.

Solution

The league ordered that the nets be measured for accuracy. Plante's charge proved correct. The goals were found to be a few inches off the required measurements. Those nets were ordered replaced with the standard Ross goals.

SECTION ONE, RULE 3b.

Comment

Art Ross was the long-time coach and general manager of

the Boston Bruins and designed the goal that today carries his name. That design includes the draping of net that replaced the rigid netting some years ago. By draping the net, the puck does not rebound out of the goal as it would if the netting were pulled tight. Until the Ross net was adopted, hometown goal judges would rarely credit a goal on a puck that banged

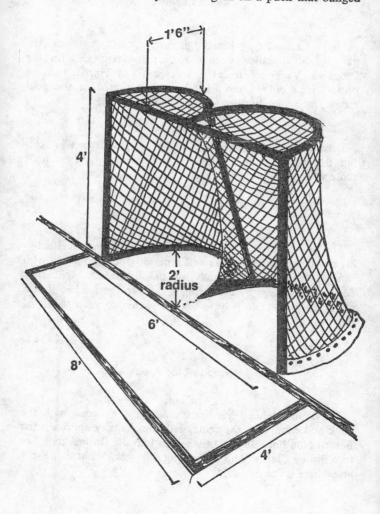

in and out of the net. Often, the home team would see to it that the net it defended for two periods had the twines drawn tight, while the one it was shooting at was nice and loose.

Goalie's Crease

Problem

Pierre Larouche of Pittsburgh turns a shot past Los Angeles goalie Rogatien Vachon for an apparent goal for the Penguins. Vachon tears after referee Wally Harris, but the protest lasts only a moment. Harris, stationed at the goal mouth, immediately rules Larouche's goal illegal.

Solution

Larouche's goal came while the Pittsburgh player was skating through Vachon's crease. An opposing player cannot score when he is in that area.

SECTION ONE, RULE 4.

Comment

The goalie's crease is 4 feet by 6 feet, and that's his turf—his sanctuary. Often goalies will remind opposing players who venture through, deliberately or unintentionally, that they don't belong there by delivering a slash to the ankles. It is a remarkably effective way to keep unwelcome visitors out of the crease.

Division of Ice Area

Problem

The Philadelphia Flyers break out of their zone with the puck and come over the center red line. As they approach the Boston blue line, Reggie Leach goes into the Bruins' zone before Bobby Clarke, who is carrying the puck. What is the call and where is the face-off?

Solution

The play is ruled offsides because the puck must always precede the attacking skater into the offensive zone. The face-off is held at the spot on the ice just outside the attacking blue line.

SECTION ONE, RULE 5.

Comment

In addition to the two blue lines, the ice is divided by a center red line. The red line runs across the neutral zone and is used to permit defending players to pass the puck out of danger without committing offsides. Besides the lines, there are 4 face-off circles (2 in each end) and 4 face-off spots in the neutral zone. Additionally, there is a center ice circle which is used only at the start of each period or after a goal has been scored. The circles have a radius of 15 feet. Years ago, there were no circles, and the referee or linesman had to use his own judgment to determine where the players should stand. The face-off spots are also a new innovation. Both the spots and circles are very important to the game and have made the officials' task in running the game much easier than it once was. They have given the game standard positions for face-offs.

Face-off "T"

Problem

Linesman Neil Armstrong whistles a Montreal rush offside and orders a face-off outside of Toronto's blue line. For the Canadiens, center Jacques Lemaire faces off against the Leafs' Darryl Sittler. Repeatedly, Lemaire reaches for the puck and goes over the restraining "T" of the face-off circle.

Solution

Armstrong orders Lemaire out of the face-off, and another Canadien skater on the ice at that moment must replace him for the draw against Sittler. If Sittler also had violated the "T" restrainer, Armstrong could order him out as well.

SECTION ONE, RULE 8a.

Comment

Referees and linesmen do not control face-offs to the extent the rule is written in the rule book. Too often, they do not make sure that the other skaters are out of the face-off circle. The introduction of the "T" painted inside of the circle has made for fairer face-offs. Before the "T" was put into use, it was common for the defending team to use a defenseman in the face-off. His only job was not to go for the puck but to take out the opposing center, tie him up, and leave the puck for his wingman to come over and pick up. Now, with the "T," the skill of the face-off man becomes very important, and you can see that with centers like Bobby Clarke, Derek Sanderson and Garry Unger.

Penalty Benches

Problem

Dave Schultz of Philadelphia and Dave Williams of Toronto collide in a corner and both players bring their sticks up. Quickly they drop their gloves and begin throwing punches. In a moment they are joined in their altercation by Ed Van Impe of the Flyers and the Leafs' Rod Seiling wrestling each other to the ice.

Solution

Schultz and Williams are penalized for 7 minutes apiece—2 minutes each for high-sticking and 5 minutes each for fighting. Van Impe and Seiling also get 5-minute majors for fighting. All four players are sent to the penalty boxes, which are separated from each other by half the length of the ice.

SECTION ONE, RULE 10a.

Comment

There was a time when NHL rinks had a single penalty box. There used to be mayhem in the single penalty box when you put two players from different teams—or four or six players—in it. To keep order, you had to have as many policemen in there as you had players.

Referee's Crease

Problem

St. Louis is trailing Minnesota by a goal in the final minute of the game. As play moves out of the St. Louis zone, goalie Gilles Gratton leaves his net, heading for the bench. But Red Berenson, the extra skater who is to replace Gratton on the ice, goes over the boards before the goalie has reached the bench. Referee Wally Harris blows his whistle signaling a Blues' penalty for having too many men on the ice. The fans scream and so do the Blues, rushing Harris on this judgment call.

Solution

Harris can retreat to his own little sanctuary—the referee's crease. That is a semicircle area 10 feet in radius drawn from the boards in front of the penalty timekeeper, and no player is allowed in there. If they cross into that crease, they are subject to misconduct penalties and heavy fines. And when a hockey player knows his beefing is going to cost money, he usually shuts up.

SECTION ONE, RULE 10b.

Comment

Years ago there was no referee's crease, and when he went

over to the penalty timekeeper to report the penalty, he had
ten or twelve players on his back to make sure that his call
was to their liking.

Signal and Timing Devices

Problem

The Chicago Black Hawks are at home against the Kansas City Scouts. With time running out in the first period, the Black Hawks are on the attack, buzzing around the Scouts' net. As the clock ticks off its final seconds, Dennis Hull shoots. The puck skids into the net as the buzzer sounds, ending the period. Is it a goal?

Solution

The answer depends on the light behind the goal. Every rink has an electrically controlled time clock. When the period ends, a green light goes on simultaneously with the buzzer or siren signaling that time has expired. When that green light goes on, it automatically cuts off the red light that would signal a goal. If the red light goes on first, then the goal counts. If the green light goes on, the red light cannot be lit, and it is no goal.

SECTION ONE, RULE 11.

Comment

There was a time when the time clock was not automatically controlled. It was a joke in those days. The clocks were often manipulated to favor the home team. Hometown timekeepers were not under the NHL's jurisdiction, and they ended the period at their own discretion. Referees had to be on the goal line at all times in order to make sure the timekeeper wasn't favoring the home team. There were plenty of battles caused by that arrangement.

Police Protection

Problem

Fans can overreact when it comes to supporting their hockey teams, and sometimes that reaction can even lead to violence. The most famous incident of this sort occurred in

1955 in Montreal. President Clarence Campbell had suspended Maurice Richard of the Canadiens after Richard attacked Boston's Hal Laycoe and punched linesman Cliff Thompson. When Campbell showed up for the next game at the Montreal Forum, the fans rioted, throwing debris at the president and even setting off tear gas bombs as the game was being played.

Solution

The game was forfeited to Detroit, which had built a 4–1 lead before the trouble began. The building was ordered emptied and angry fans swarmed through Montreal's downtown area, looting stores, overturning trolleys, and doing more than $100,000 in damage. Police arrested forty persons.

SECTION ONE, RULE 12.

Comment

I drew the refereeing assignment for the next game in the Forum. For protection, they had mounted policemen riding up and down the aisles of the building to make certain there was no repeat of the rowdyism. Now there is a rule in the book that requires NHL teams to provide adequate police or other protection for the players and officials, and all rinks comply. Believe me, it is the best rule they ever put in that book.

Section 2
THE TEAMS

Hockey is played by two teams, each using 5 skaters and a goalie when they are full strength. But the composition of those teams can be a complex matter.

The NHL rules now limit clubs to 17 skaters in uniform and 2 goalies. That player limit has gone up and down over the years, but 17 seems to be the best number. Most teams use three regular lines, accounting for 9 forwards, and rotate 5 of 6 defensemen. That takes care of 15 players. The other 2 are usually spare forwards, used to kill penalties or to form a fourth skating line with one of the other players, who takes a double shift.

College rules permit 18 skaters—usually 6 defensemen and 12 forwards. Any more than that and some of the players simply wouldn't get any ice time at all.

Skaters are permitted to change "on the fly"—that is, while the action continues. I have always felt that this is one of the most exciting aspects of hockey. In youth hockey, however, that rule is suspended.

In rinks that have intramural programs—called house leagues—there are certain adjustments to the accepted rules on teams. For example, the kids who play in my rink in New Hyde Park, New York, are broken up into 15-player teams. That gives their coaches three complete line shifts of 5 players each. They are balanced out with each team getting one first line of 5 stronger players, a second line of 5 mediocre players, and a third line of 5 weaker skaters. The strongest lines play against each other for two minutes. Then the second lines oppose each other for two minutes. Then the third lines go for two minutes. No changes are permitted and this assures a balanced game—something the administrators of the program are most interested in.

Other youth leagues, I'm sure, have their own methods of assuring parity between their teams.

Each team has a single player designated as its captain. He and he alone is permitted to discuss with the referee any questions regarding interpretation of rules. If he comes over to the referee to discuss any other aspect of the game, it can cost him a misconduct penalty. That is a stiff new rule adopted before the 1975 season to back the officials, and it's one that was about twenty years too late to help me. When I was refereeing in the NHL, I had a dozen or so helpers from each team, all of them anxious to assist me in my calls—whether I wanted them to or not.

Uniforms

Problem

The New York Islanders are at home against the New York Rangers. Pete Stemkowski of the Rangers pulls down the Islanders' Clark Gillies with a hook, and referee Bruce Hood blows his whistle for the penalty. Now Hood skates to the timekeeper to report the penalty. Obviously, he can't identify either player with the team designation "New York." Both are playing for New York. Neither do officials use team nicknames. So how does Hood announce the penalties?

Solution

Officials use uniform colors to identify the players on the ice. The Rangers wear blue on the road, so Hood's call would be "No. 21, Blue, two minutes, hooking."

SECTION TWO, RULE 13b.

Comment

All NHL teams wear white uniforms at home and colored uniforms on the road. And all the colors are easily identifiable and unique. In the old six-team league, the Rangers and Toronto always wore blue jerseys. The Detroit Red Wings and Montreal Canadiens always wore red and the Boston Bruins and Chicago Black Hawks always wore black. That made the game confusing for everybody in the building, including the players. It certainly made for a better hockey game when they distinguished the teams by making the home club wear the light uniform and the visitors wear the dark.

Captains

Problem

Referee Bob Meyers makes a disputed call against the Montreal Canadiens, whistling defenseman Serge Savard off the ice for boarding Marcel Dionne of Los Angeles. The Montreal Forum crowd moans at the call, and Savard chases after Meyers protesting the referee's decision.

Solution

Unless Savard wants to get himself a misconduct, he'd better back away. He has no business discussing the referee's call with Meyers. That job belongs to only one Montreal player, the team's captain, Yvan Cournoyer.

SECTION TWO, RULE 14.

Comment

Years ago teams also had captains, but that didn't mean anything because everybody on the ice would come up and start arguing with the referee after a penalty or any other call. Sometimes, the coach would call the referee over to the bench, and if the official was silly enough to go over there, he'd be berated by the coach as well. Under the rule adopted in 1975, each team will have only one player, the designated captain, who can talk with the referee. And if the referee is abused, he can assess a 2-minute penalty. What's more, the rule states that the captain may only talk to the referee "relating to interpretation of the rules." It does not say "relating to judgment," and the rule specifically calls for a misconduct penalty to be imposed should the referee's judgment be questioned. It is difficult to enforce this rule, but it is up to the referee to set his standard early in the season and stick by it.

Lineups

Problem

The Chicago Black Hawks were carrying several extra players on a road trip. All of them warmed up, but when Coach Billy Reay made out his roster for that night's game, he inadvertently left off the list the name of star left wing Dennis Hull. "Just an oversight," said Reay. "Here, let me fix it."

Solution

Sorry, Billy. Once the lineup is submitted, it is considered official—mistakes and all. No changes are allowed, and even though he was healthy and perfectly capable of playing, Hull had to sit out the game because of Reay's oversight.

SECTION TWO, RULE 15a.

Comment

When the coaches submit their lineups of the 17 skaters they will use, it is final and no deviations are permitted. Reay's mistake was caused because of the extra bodies the Black Hawks had with them. The coach can lose track and make a costly mistake. But it's a cinch that after this happened to a smart coach like Reay, it would never happen to him a second time.

Players in Uniform

Problem

In a game in New York a few years ago, St. Louis goalie

Glenn Hall, usually a rather placid fellow, got thrown out for beefing to the referee. Then his replacement, Robbie Irons, suffered an injury. What does the St. Louis club do for a goaltender now?

Solution

Fortunately for the Blues, they were carrying 3 goalies on their roster at the time. So Jacques Plante, seated in the stands, rushed downstairs to the dressing room and replaced Irons. He played a shutout that night.

SECTION TWO, RULE 15d and e.

Comment

Only a few teams carry 3 goalies. Most feel 2 is sufficient. In the event both goalies are injured and the team does not have a third man available, one of the other players on the team would have to play goal. That is the only time a player other than a goaltender is permitted to wear a goalie's equipment. Years ago, teams carried only 1 goalie, and if he was injured, the home team had to supply a standby. In Detroit, the standby goalie was the Red Wings' trainer, Lefty Wilson. He was pretty good at it and, in fact, came off the bench to beat his own team a few times.

Starting Lineup

Problem

Buffalo is playing at home against New York. The Rangers' starting lineup is announced with Phil Esposito's line. The Sabres decide to start Don Luce's line, figuring that Luce is a top defensive center who can keep Esposito in check. The Rangers don't want this and pull Esposito's line back before the opening face-off, attempting to substitute Pete Stemkowski's line. What is the ruling?

Solution

Esposito's line must start the game. The home team has the

option of naming its lineup after the visitors, and the lineups submitted must be followed. New York can make its change as soon as play begins if it wishes.

SECTION TWO, RULE 16b.

Comment

Forcing the visiting team to name its lineup first is the only advantage the home team has in the game of hockey. It allows the home team to respond with the players and lines it feels are best suited to handling the visitors' lineup. Pairings are vital, and coaches are always trying to get the edge on the other team in that area. The referee always must allow the home team the option of making the final change of skaters, not only at the start of a period but prior to any face-off as well. That's why you will often see referees order certain skaters off the ice before a face-off, ruling that the visiting team may not make any more changes.

Changing Players

Problem

Atlanta and California are playing, and there is a long period of time without any whistle. As play continues, the two teams find it necessary to change skaters and get fresh legs on the ice. How is it accomplished?

Solution

The two teams change "on the fly"—that is, while play continues. Usually, when this occurs, a team changes one skater at a time with a fresh center going over the boards as the other center comes off the ice, etc.

SECTION TWO, RULE 18.

Comment

The thing that makes hockey as fast and as enjoyable as it is, is being able to change players on the fly without any halt in the action. Some coaches are better at doing this than others. It is the player's responsibility to be ready to come over the bench when the player he is to replace heads for the bench. Officials give a certain amount of leeway in the changing on the fly. You are allowed to change if you are at the bench and out of the play. That's why some players will skate right past the puck at the sideboards. If they are changing and touch the puck, their team could be penalized for too many men on the ice. Different referees have different interpretations of what constitutes being out of the play and eligible to change.

Pulling the Goalie

Problem

In the Stanley Cup semifinal play-offs a couple of years ago, the New York Rangers were trailing Philadelphia, 4–3, in the final minute of the seventh game. The Rangers wanted to lift goalie Ed Giacomin for an extra attacker. New York's extra skater, in his anxiety, rushed into the play. Anything wrong with that?

Solution

The new man did not wait long enough for Giacomin to reach the players' bench. Linesman John D'Amico noticed the infraction and called it to the attention of the referee who imposed the too-many-men-on-the-ice penalty, ending the Rangers' chances.

SECTION TWO, RULE 18a.

Comment

This is one of the best rules put into the book, and one that is called very solidly by officials around the NHL. Years ago, the goalie would head for the bench and once he got to within 20 or 30 feet, his replacement would be over the boards and on the ice. Now they call this play very closely, and teams can't take liberties with the rule. You can compare the change of players on the fly in hockey with football's two-minute offense which is designed to move the club downfield quickly in a minimum amount of time. The change is practiced very often in hockey so that the mistakes aren't made. The rule is strict, and if it results in a penalty being imposed, it can mean the hockey game.

Too Many Men on the Ice

Problem

Atlanta, playing in New York, trailed the Rangers by one goal late in the third period. Bernie Geoffrion, then coach of the Flames, lifted goalie Dan Bouchard in the final minute. But instead of one Flame skater replacing Bouchard, two players took the ice, one joining Atlanta's attack on the New York net and the other, defenseman Pat Quinn, hanging back near the neutral zone.

Solution

The Flames were called for too many men on the ice when Quinn blocked a Ranger shot that was heading for the empty Atlanta net. The violation probably wouldn't have been noticed if Quinn had not blocked the shot and become obvious.

SECTION TWO, RULE 18b.

Comment

Geoffrion said that he learned that trick under Toe Blake with the Montreal Canadiens. Blake said the ruse was rarely noticed with all of the action in front of the net, and you could often get away with seven skaters instead of six in the final minute after pulling your goalie. But, if you get caught, as Geoffrion did, and there isn't enough time to serve the penalty, a deliberate violation like that can call for a penalty shot.

Injured Goalies

Problem

The St. Louis Blues are on the attack and pressuring

Buffalo goalie Gerry Desjardins. He makes half a dozen saves and then falls to the ice, apparently injured. He leaves the ice and Gary Bromley replaces him. The Sabres request time to warm up the new goalie. What is the referee's ruling?

Solution

No warm-up is allowed. The reserve goalie must go right into the nets and play must be resumed immediately. What's more, the injured goalie may not return to the game until the first stoppage of play after the resumption of action.

SECTION TWO, RULE 19b.

Comment

Many teams made it a practice to have their goalies fake an injury in order to get a stoppage of play and perhaps halt an attacking team's momentum. If a team was getting pounded and the players needed a rest, the goalie would come up with some fictitious injury. That would delay the game and was an irritation for the spectators and an advantage for the goalkeeper and the team that caused the delay. With the rule the way it is now written, it hardly pays the team to feign an injury.

Injured Players

Problem

Montreal's Guy Lafleur goes into the corner against Stan Mikita of Chicago. Their sticks come up and both players are called for high-sticking. Mikita suffers a cut over his eye in the exchange and must go to the trainer's room for some stitches. How is his penalty time served?

Solution

Another player is designated to sit in the penalty box, replacing Mikita. When Mikita's penalty time is completed, his stand-in may leave the box. However, should Mikita's treatment be completed before his penalty time is over, he cannot return to the ice. Instead, he must go to the penalty box, replacing the teammate who was serving time in his place.

SECTION TWO, RULE 19e.

Comment

This is where a coach can be very important. He has to be careful in selecting the player he wants to sit out the penalty time for an injured teammate, or in the case of a bench minor. The player in the penalty box may be in a position to join in the play when the penalty time is up, so it is important that the coach weigh his choice carefully. For example, you wouldn't send a defenseman to the box to serve a center's penalty time. If you did, when the time expired, you'd have that defenseman joining the two already on the ice and it could cause confusion.

When to Whistle

Problem

Washington's Bill Clement collides with Vic Hadfield of Pittsburgh near center ice. The puck is loose and recovered by the Penguins' Pierre Larouche, who starts up ice with it. But Hadfield is hurt. He's still down on the ice as play continues. What should the referee do?

Solution

The rule book says that play should be continued until the injured player's team gains control of the puck. Then the referee should blow his whistle. That way, a feigned injury would not penalize the opposing team. An exception is when the injured player's team has a scoring opportunity or the injury sustained is obviously serious. In the first exception, the referee allows the play to be completed. In the second, he blows his whistle immediately, regardless of which team has control of the puck.

SECTION TWO, RULE 19f.

Comment

The referee carries a lot of responsibility here. Besides being a referee and judge, he's got to have some medical knowledge as well. Overall, however, this is a good rule because it cuts down on the number of faked injuries.

Section 3
THE EQUIPMENT

A hockey player's equipment is the key to his trade and often can determine his success or failure on the ice. That's why the players are so fussy about their gear.

Essentially, players at every level of hockey use the same basic equipment—skates, sticks, shin guards, elbow pads, and heavy gauntlet-type gloves.

There are, however, a couple of very vital differences between the equipment required in collegiate and youth hockey and the accessories that a professional must use. The differences involve perhaps the most important piece of equipment a hockey player can have. That is a helmet. College players and youngsters getting started in hockey are not permitted on the ice without headgear. Professionals leave helmets to the option of the individual players.

Someday, I think, helmets and mouthpieces will be mandatory in the pro leagues the same as they are elsewhere in hockey. It is only sensible that if players go to such extreme lengths to protect other parts of their bodies, they should take the very basic, simple step of wearing a helmet to protect the most vital part of their bodies.

It's much the same as goaltenders' masks. They are not required in pro hockey, but now that Gump Worsley has retired, there are no more than one or two goalies in all the pro leagues who don't wear masks.

More and more players coming into pro ranks are wearing helmets, simply because they've learned their hockey that way and are perfectly comfortable with that piece of equipment. Older players, who grew up without helmets and never were able to adjust to them when they became popular, are slowly drifting out of the game.

Players are very particular about their equipment. Skates must be sharpened to individual tastes, and sticks are tailored individually.

Every player has a half-dozen or so of his personal sticks on hand for every game. The sticks are tailor-made to each player's personal specifications, but they never seem satisfied with them. After a player receives his supply of woods from the manufacturer, he manicures them meticulously. He heats them with acetylene torches. He shapes them. He planes them. He saws them. But if you ask me, most of that stuff is strictly psychological. It's all in their heads.

The Blade

Problem

When he played in the NHL, Bobby Hull had a curved blade on the end of his hockey stick that made his already awesome slap shot one of the most dangerous weapons in the history of hockey. When Hull's hooked blade connected on his slap shot, the puck would soar and dip crazily. "How can you stop that thing?" asked one angry goalie. "You never know where it's going. It's like trying to catch a knuckleball that's going a hundred miles an hour. The damned thing is going to kill somebody one of these days."

Solution

Eventually, legislation was adopted, restricting the curvature of the stick's blade to one-half inch—quite a bit less than the hook Hull was using.

SECTION THREE, RULE 20b.

Comment

At one time there was no such thing as a curved stick. A stick was either left-handed, right-handed, or neutral. Bobby Hull and Stan Mikita brought the curved sticks into the game, bending their blades under the door of the dressing room. That development made shots much more important than the old arts of stickhandling and playmaking. Sticks today also are much lighter than ever before. Hockey players have gotten away from the use of heavy tape on the blades. They once thought the tape helped control the puck. Now they feel they're better off with less tape and a lighter stick that gives them a better feel of the puck.

Sticks

Problem

Coach Billy Reay on the Chicago Black Hawks' bench complains that an opposing player is using an illegal stick. He demands that it be measured. The request is made formally by the Black Hawks' captain to the referee.

Solution

Besides his whistle, every referee carries with him a tape measure just for this kind of situation. There are rigid standards on stick size. The rule book says no stick should exceed 55 inches in length from heel to the end of the shaft or more than 12½ inches from the heel to the end of the blade. A goalie's stick may not exceed 3½ inches in width except at the heel, where it may not exceed 4½ inches. The regular player's blade may not be more than 3 inches in width or less than 2 inches. The distance from the heel to the end of the blade on a goalie's stick may not exceed 15½ inches.

SECTION THREE, RULE 20b.

Comment

There have been tremendous changes in sticks in the history of hockey. At one time there were no restrictions. Some hockey players made great reputations as checkers and were artists with the stick. One in particular was the great Hall of Famer Frank Nighbor. They said his stick was 10 feet long and, of course, that gave him quite an advantage.

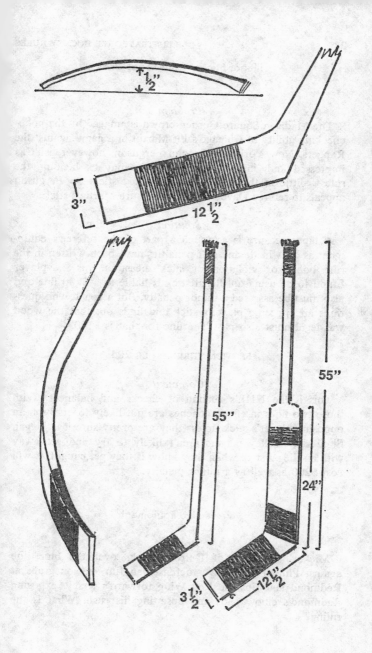

Illegal Sticks—and Legal Ones

Problem

The Madison Square Garden crowd is amazed by the poke-checking ability of Chicago's Pit Martin in a game against the Rangers. New York Coach John Ferguson, however, isn't as impressed and, in fact, thinks Martin may be bending the rules a little in the length of his hockey stick. So Ferguson appeals to referee Dave Newell to measure Martin's stick.

Solution

A tape measure is as much a part of the referee's equipment as his whistle and stiff penalties have been written in the rule book for violation of stick measurements. A player found to be using an illegal stick is liable to a $200 fine and also must be assessed a minor penalty. But a coach who questions an opposing player's stick and finds out that the wood was legal must also pay. The fine for that is $100.

SECTION THREE, RULE 20d.

Comment

This is the NHL's version of checks and balances. With those two fines in effect, coaches are not likely to question an opposing player's stick unless they are pretty sure it is illegal. Similarly, hockey players aren't likely to try and get away with an illegal stick when they know if they get caught, it will cost $200 as well as a minor penalty.

Protective Equipment

Problem

Mickey Redmond of Detroit breaks over the blue line against Philadelphia. Flyer defenseman Jim Watson grabs at Redmond and rips the Red Wing forward's jersey, exposing Redmond's elbow pads and upsetting his rush. What is the ruling?

Solution

Watson is sent off for holding, and Redmond must get a new jersey. He cannot play with his protective equipment exposed because it can pose an injury hazard to other players on the ice. If Redmond plays without changing jerseys, he is liable to a minor penalty.

SECTION THREE, RULE 23.

Comment

It wasn't so very long ago that players were permitted to wear protective equipment like elbow and knee pads outside of their uniforms. They created a number of injuries, which was the reason for the rule change requiring that such gear be worn under the uniform. I'd be remiss here if while discussing protective equipment, I didn't mention helmets. The NHL has no rule requiring helmets, but it really should. They are required in every collegiate and junior hockey league across the United States and Canada, and because that's where younger players develop you find more and more helmets being worn in the NHL voluntarily. But they should be mandatory in view of the kind of protection they provide.

Dangerous Equipment

Problem

A few years ago, Chicago was trailing the New York Rangers by a goal late in a game. Coach Billy Reay, looking for any edge he could get, called the attention of referee Art Skov to Ranger forward Glen Sather's glove which had the palm worn away and Sather's fingers showing through it.

Solution

Skov ordered Sather to the penalty box for 2 minutes for playing with illegal equipment. The power play didn't pay off for the Black Hawks, but Reay had displayed a smart piece of coaching. He had noticed the violation in the first period

but waited until it was to Chicago's best advantage to point
it out to the referee.

Comment

The palmless glove is an old trick that was used to the
greatest extent by the Toronto Maple Leafs when Hap Day
coached that team. Usually the Leafs would cut the palms out
of their defensemen's gloves. That way, when they were lean-
ing up against an opposing player it would look as if they
were just hanging their hands there but at the same time, they
were grabbing hold of the pants. That's how they came to be
known as the clutch-and-grab club. The glove must have a
full palm so that the fingers cannot be put outside of it.

The Puck

Problem

Garry Unger of St. Louis and Marcel Dionne of Los Angeles are two of the NHL's best puck handlers. Yet both
center-ice men are experiencing difficulty in this game. The
puck keeps bouncing on them and they are unable to control
it for more than a stride or two. They complain to the referee.

Solution

Most likely, the puck has not been frozen sufficiently. The
home team is required to supply the pucks for each game and
the trainer or equipment man freezes a bucketful a couple of
hours before game time. A frozen puck provides better control for the players and doesn't hop around like a rubber
ball.

Comment

The puck has undergone important changes over the years.

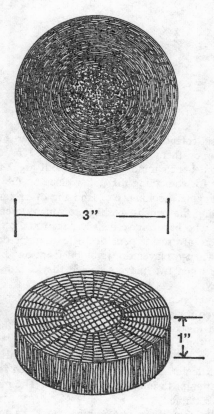

It used to be that the puck did not have a beveled edge. It was quite sharp causing a lot of injuries to hockey players. Beside preventing injuries, the beveled edge helps the puck lie flat on the ice and not roll so much.

Section 4
PENALTIES

There are six categories of penalties that a referee can call, although two of them really could be listed as one—minor penalties and bench minor penalties. Both are 2-minute sentences, one for something that takes place on the ice, such as holding, tripping, hooking, etc., and the other for an infraction involving the bench—perhaps too many men on the ice or a coach who has to have his say once too often.

Then there are major penalties of 5 minutes duration that are given when a player draws blood from another or, more frequently, when two players decide they'd rather box than play hockey.

Misconduct penalties carry 10-minute sentences and are usually given for a player mouthing off to a referee. A player receiving a misconduct also is fined $50, and that fine goes up to $100 for a game misconduct.

A match penalty, like a game misconduct, finishes a player for that particular game and usually is imposed for deliberate injury or attempt to injure another player. The match penalty carries a $200 fine.

A penalty shot is, in my opinion, hockey's most exciting confrontation—the one-on-one match up of shooter and goalie. It can be called for a variety of violations but the most frequent is fouling from behind a skater who will have a clear shot on the goalie.

Minor penalties terminate if a goal is scored by the team enjoying the manpower advantage. Major penalties must be served for the full 5-minute term, no matter how many goals are scored during that time. If two players engage in a fight and go off together for 5-minute majors, their teams are not shorthanded and maintain their full skating complement of men during that time. The same is true of misconducts, which are strictly personal penalties and do not reduce the skating strength of the penalized player's team.

Every penalty has a specific signal that the referee uses to identify the violation to everybody in the arena. Those signals, well-known in hockey, were devised by me, and for a very simple reason. I didn't know what else to do with my hands when I started refereeing, so I decided to use them that way. When I started the signals, they were strictly informal. But they must have been a good idea because they were later adopted as official.

Serving Penalties

Problem

Cliff Koroll of the Chicago Black Hawks trips Philadelphia Bill Barber. Referee Dave Newell raises his arm to signal the penalty but does not blow his whistle because the Flyers are still in control of the puck. Barber regains his balance and continues his rush as goalie Bernie Parent hurries off to give Philadelphia an extra skater on the delayed penalty. Now Phil Russell grabs Barber and the Black Hawks gain control of the puck. Newell assesses two minor penalties against Chicago, the first to Koroll for tripping and the second to Russell for holding. Both are reported to the penalty timekeeper at the same time. When the Flyers score on the power play, who returns to the ice first, Koroll or Russell?

Solution

Chicago's captain, Stan Mikita, must indicate to the penalty timekeeper which player should exit the box first. If the Hawks do not designate one or the other, the timekeeper decides on his own.

SECTION FOUR, RULE 27.

Comment

This is an important function of the captain that should not be overlooked. In the case cited, the Hawks would probably prefer getting Russell back first to bolster their defense since they will still be short one man. Koroll is a forward and more easily replaced on the ice than a defenseman like Russell.

Minor Penalties

Problem

The New York Islanders are defending against a Philadelphia rush. Mel Bridgman of the Flyers sidesteps Islander defenseman Denis Potvin, who hooks him. Referee Bryan Lewis calls the penalty, and Potvin goes off for 2 minutes. Thirty seconds into his penalty, the Flyers score. What happens to Potvin now?

Solution

Potvin immediately leaves the penalty box, restoring the Islanders to full strength. He would only stay in the box following a Philadelphia goal if he were serving a major penalty for cutting Bridgman.

SECTION FOUR, RULE 27.

Comment

Until the mid-1950s, minor penalties meant that a hockey player stayed off the ice for the full 2 minutes and his team played shorthanded for that entire span, no matter how often the other team scored. That was changed because of the Montreal Canadiens who had perhaps the greatest power play in the history of hockey. The Canadiens used Doug Harvey and Boom Boom Geoffrion on the points with Maurice Richard, Jean Beliveau, and Dickie Moore up front. It was not unusual during the course of a single minor penalty for this awesome power play to come up with two, three, or even four goals. If this happened early in a game, the game for all practical purposes was over, and the ones who really suffered were the people who paid the tab—the fans. As a result, the rule was changed, and I think the change was a good one.

Major and Minor Penalties

Problem

Dallas Smith of Boston boards Toronto's George Ferguson and referee Ron Wicks sees the infraction. But before Wicks can assess it, Ferguson and Smith drop their gloves and start fighting. When the fisticuffs end, Wicks doles out 7 penalty minutes to Smith—a major for fighting and the original minor for boarding. Ferguson draws 5 minutes for fighting. Which of Smith's penalties is served first, the major or the minor?

Solution

Smith and Ferguson serve their major penalties first and then Smith serves his minor, giving Toronto its power-play advantage at the end of his penalty term.

SECTION FOUR, RULE 28.

Comment

The reason for this is that Ferguson, the man Smith fouled, will be able to return to the ice and take advantage of the Bruins' shorthanded situation. The coincident major penalties merely delay Boston's shorthanded situation.

Mariucci's Misconduct

Problem

Johnny Mariucci is one of the most respected men in hockey circles and is credited with helping build the Minnesota North Stars franchise. But when he played hockey for the Chicago Black Hawks, he was a terror on the ice. One night, I caught Mariucci holding and gave him a 2-minute penalty. Johnny ranted and raved and the Chicago Stadium fans loved every moment of it. One of them dropped a deck of cards on the ice while Mariucci kept complaining. He was playing to them and they were responding, and unless I did something fast, the whole scene was going to get completely out of hand.

Solution

I picked up the cards, which had landed in front of the penalty box, and skated over to where Mariucci was bellowing. I handed the cards to him and said, "Here, John, you can use these for a game of solitaire because you just got ten more minutes for misconduct."

SECTION FOUR, RULE 29.

Comment

That was the last thing I heard from Mr. Mariucci that night. The misconduct penalty can be a referee's best weapon if he uses it properly.

Third Man in Misconduct

Problem

Barclay Plager of the St. Louis Blues gets into a fight with Ab Demarco of Vancouver. Demarco is getting the best of the fight when suddenly Plager's brother, Bob, jumps into it, pulling the Canuck player off Barclay. Linesmen John D'Amico and Matt Pavelich quickly move in to separate the players. Now referee Andy van Hellemond must dole out the penalties. What is his call?

Problem

Barclay Plager and Demarco both get 5-minute major penalties for fighting. But Bob Plager is through for the night, tagged with a game misconduct for being the third man in the fight.

SECTION FOUR, RULE 29d.

Comment

The third-man-in rule is one of the best ones ever written. Because it is so severe, players hesitate to jump into fights. In the past, fights between two players often developed into bench-clearing brawls. Now, players don't join in the battle,

and that makes it much easier for the officials to end the fight
and get the hockey game resumed.

Misconduct Penalties

Problem

Goalie Cesare Maniago of Minnesota complains vehemently
to the referee over a disputed goal that Maniago claims did
not completely cross the goal line. When Maniago prolongs
his protest, he is assessed a misconduct penalty. How is it
served?

Solution

Goalies are the only players on the team not required to
serve their own penalty time. Instead, Minnesota coach Ted
Harris must designate another skater to spend 10 minutes in
the penalty box. The North Stars, however, are not short-
handed during that period.

SECTION FOUR, RULES 29 and 31.

Comment

Misconducts cost players $50. A game misconduct carries
a $100 fine. Also, it should be noted that players are not
allowed out at the precise moment that 10 minutes have
elapsed on the clock. They must wait until the next stoppage
of play. That means a 10-minute misconduct penalty can
really stretch to 11 or 12 minutes if there are no halts in
the action.

Match Penalties

Problem

Montreal's Maurice "Rocket" Richard was one of the most
hot-tempered players in the history of hockey. The Rocket
was highly competitive and stopped at nothing when he was
on the ice. I remember one game during the play-offs when

the Canadiens were playing the Toronto Maple Leafs. Bill Ezinicki, later a professional golfer but in those days one of the Maple Leafs' mainstays, was hounding Richard. The Rocket decided the solution would be to part Ezinicki's hair, and he used his stick to do the job.

Solution

I gave Richard a match penalty for deliberately attempting to injure Ezinicki. In the 20 minutes that Montreal had to play shorthanded because of the penalty, Toronto scored enough goals to win the game. In those days, a match penalty also carried automatic suspension from the next game, and without Richard, the Canadiens were beaten again and eliminated from the play-offs.

SECTION FOUR, RULE 30.

Comment

The rules have been altered some since the Richard-Ezinicki affair. Now, an attempt to injure calls for a match penalty with the penalized team playing shorthanded for 5 minutes. A deliberate injury costs a match penalty and 10 minutes shorthanded. There is not, however, any automatic suspension as well, although suspensions are often added by the league president after he reviews the case.

Penalty Shot

Problem

Defenseman Gary Bergman of the Kansas City Scouts falls on the puck in the crease of his team's goal net, preventing a shot by Pittsburgh's Vic Hadfield and halting a Penguin attack on the Scouts. Referee Bryan Lewis immediately blows his whistle. What is the call?

Solution

Lewis awards a penalty shot to the Penguins. Pittsburgh can designate any of the players on the ice at the time of the

infraction to take the shot. Falling on the puck in the crease is one of several actions that calls for penalty shots. Others include throwing a stick at an attacking player, fouling a player from behind when he has clear access to a shot on goal, deliberately displacing the goalpost, and picking up the puck in the crease area.

SECTION FOUR, RULE 31.

Comment

At one time there were two ways to take a penalty shot. One of them involved a line drawn across the ice some 30 feet from the goal line. The puck would have to be shot from beyond that line under certain penalty-shot conditions. Other penalty shots were set up as they are today, with the puck on the center red line. In my opinion, more penalty shots should be called and it would be better for the game if referees would take the initiative and call more of them. It is the most exciting play in hockey, and I must admit that when I refereed, I didn't call as many as I should have.

Penalty-shot Penalties

Problem

The Boston Bruins' slick center Jean Ratelle intercepts a Montreal pass in the center-ice zone and all alone bursts in on goalie Ken Dryden. Canadiens' defender Larry Robinson, recovering late, chases Ratelle, and just as Jean is about to launch his shot, Robinson pulls him down from behind. Referee Ron Wicks blows his whistle.

Solution

Wicks' proper call is for a penalty shot since Ratelle was fouled from behind and would have had a clear shot on goal if Robinson had not interrupted him.

SECTION FOUR, RULE 31.

Comment

Ratelle gets 1 shot—no rebounds allowed—as a result of Robinson's infraction. But not too many years ago, the penalty shot was more severe. If the penalty shot was missed, the

offending player—in this case Montreal's Robinson—still had
to serve the penalty time in the box, leaving his team short-
handed. I guess the rule was changed because that constituted
double jeopardy.

Penalty-shot Advantage

Problem

Buffalo's Rick Martin is pulled down from behind on a
breakaway against the Detroit Red Wings. Referee Wally

Harris signals for a penalty shot, and both teams leave the ice with only Martin and Red Wing goalie Ed Giacomin remaining. Now Harris must give each player the penalty shot instructions. What are they?

Solution

Basically, the rules covering penalty shots are quite simple. The puck is placed at center ice and the shooter picks it up there and makes his move on the net. He is permitted 1 shot with no rebounds allowed. The goalie must stay in his crease until the shooter picks up the puck. After that, it's one-on-one, and may the best man win.

SECTION FOUR, RULE 31.

Comment

Goalies have become so proficient that they now seem to hold the edge in penalty-shot showdowns. It used to be that hockey people felt the shooter had a 70 per cent chance of scoring on a penalty shot. Now that has been reversed, and most goalies figure that 70 per cent chance is in favor of them stopping the shot. In some cases, the player awarded the penalty shot could be a defenseman who is not accustomed to stickhandling or shooting the puck. In such cases, the penalized team probably would prefer the risk of a penalty shot instead of a 2-minute shorthanded situation created by an ordinary minor penalty.

Picking the Penalty Shooter

Problem

Detroit and the New York Rangers were battling for a play-off spot in 1961. In a late-season game, the score was tied, 2–2, when Dean Prentice broke down the left side of the ice. Red Wing goalie Hank Bassen lost control of his stick and it flew out of his hands and struck Prentice as the Ranger was closing in for a shot. Referee Eddie Powers blew his whistle. What is the call?

Solution

Powers properly ruled a penalty shot because Bassen had thrown his stick at the attacking player. But then the referee made a mistake, allowing Andy Bathgate to take the shot instead of Prentice, who was the player fouled.

SECTION FOUR, RULE 31c.

Comment

There are strict rules about who takes penalty shots. When a player is fouled, that player is supposed to take the shot. When an infraction like falling on the puck in the crease causes the penalty shot, the team awarded the shot may select a player on the ice at the time of the infraction to take the shot. Powers confused that rule. Bathgate scored on the shot, giving the Rangers the victory and helping them nail down that play-off spot.

Goalkeeper-Referee Rapport

Problem

Dave Gardner of California trips Vancouver's Paulin Bordeleau and goes to the penalty box for 2 minutes. While the Seals are trying to kill off the penalty, goalie Gilles Meloche does a little tripping of his own on Vancouver's John Gould.

Solution

Technically, the referee should call all penalties the same way. You establish a standard early in the game, and you stick by it. That's how a referee earns respect in the National Hockey League. But don't be surprised if, in this case, Meloche gets away with his violation.

SECTION FOUR, RULE 32.

Comment

There has always been a certain rapport between goalkeepers and referees. They are both harassed at one time or another, the goalkeeper by pucks and the referee by mouths. I think referees are more likely to overlook a violation by a goalie than by another player. So goalies have always gotten away with a tremendous amount of things—tripping, interference, slashing. Some goalies even come out of the net to do their thing. They get away with murder, but it's always been that way.

The Roving Goalie

Problem

Goalie John Davidson of the New York Rangers circles behind his net to cut off a loose puck. He is checked hard by Toronto's Dave Williams, who ignores one of hockey's unwritten rules about hitting the goalie. As Williams pursues the puck, New York's Carol Vadnais boards the Maple Leaf skater and the two begin throwing punches. In a moment, Davidson, still angry about being hit, skates in to join the fight.

Solution

Depending on the first check and whether it was legal or not, Williams could have gotten a penalty for tagging Davidson. Certainly, he and Vadnais must go off for their fight and Vadnais could get an extra minor, depending on whether he boarded Williams legally or not. Davidson gets a minor penalty for leaving his crease during an altercation and also could get a game misconduct as the third man in the fight between Vadnais and Williams. Davidson is also liable to be fined for his act.

SECTION FOUR, RULE 32.

Comment

In today's rule book, goalies are liable for as many penalties as forwards or defensemen. Many of them, like passing the red line, seem innocent. But it's all for the goalie's protection. It's also for the protection of the owners and operators of the hockey club. Money to pay fines is easy to acquire. Goalies are not.

Goalkeeper Penalties

Problem

Goalie Gary Smith of Vancouver gets involved in a fight with Chicago's Stan Mikita in the first period of a game between the Canucks and Black Hawks. In the second period, Smith fights Chicago's John Marks, and in the third period, it's Smith vs. Keith Magnuson of the Hawks. What are the penalties?

Solution

For each of the first two fights, Smith gets major penalties and the 5 minutes in the penalty box must be served by a teammate. The third major, however, calls for the goalie's expulsion from the game and an automatic fine of $100.

SECTION FOUR, RULE 32c.

Comment

As in the case of minor penalties, goaltenders' majors must be served by a player who was on the ice at the time of the infraction. Goalies wear 40 pounds or so of bulky equipment and rarely get involved in one fight, let alone three of them in a single game.

Multiple Penalties

Problem

Pete Mahovlich of Montreal trips Atlanta's Tom Lysiak, giving the Flames a power play. Ten seconds later, the infraction is repeated, this time with penalty-killer Jimmy Roberts tripping Bill Flett and getting sent off to join Mahovlich in the penalty box. With the 2-man advantage, the

Flames score a goal. Who returns to the ice, Mahovlich or Roberts?

Solution

The first man in is the first man out. Thus, even though the Flames' goal came on a 2-man advantage, only one Canadien skater, Mahovlich, returns following the goal. Roberts must serve the balance of his penalty, unless the Flames score again.

SECTION FOUR, RULE 33.

Comment

This rule puts a great burden on the penalty timekeeper. Often a team will have three, four or even five men in the penalty box, serving time. Ice strength can never fall below three skaters, but that doesn't limit the number of penalties a referee can call. They become delayed penalties with the time being served in order of the penalties. The timekeeper has to be an accountant to know who leaves the box, and when he leaves.

Delayed Penalties

Problem

André Boudrias of Vancouver is pulled down by the Rangers' Steve Vickers, but the Canucks retain control of the puck and continue to attack the New York net. Referee Bob Meyers has his arm in the air, indicating the penalty on Vickers. When does he blow his whistle?

Solution

He must wait until the Canucks have lost control of the puck to the Rangers. If he blows it immediately, he deprives Vancouver of a scoring opportunity and gives an advantage to New York, the team that committed the infraction.

SECTION FOUR, RULE 34 a and b.

Comment

Every referee makes a mistake, and this rule caused one of my worst ones. During a Stanley Cup play-off game between Montreal and Boston, Doug Harvey of the Canadiens pulled down the Bruins' Milt Schmidt. Boston never lost the puck, but I lost my poise and blew the whistle just as the Bruins scored a goal. I had to disallow it, and I also had to apologize to Boston coach Lynn Patrick. Mistakes—that's why they put erasers on the ends of pencils.

"Washed Out" Penalties

Problem

Boston's Jean Ratelle takes a pass from Johnny Bucyk and sidesteps defenseman Bob Gassoff of St. Louis. The Blues' Ted Irvine hooks Ratelle, but the Bruin center shakes off the violation and continues toward the net. Referee John McCauley, seeing the penalty, raises his arm, but does not blow his whistle because Ratelle is still in control of the puck. Goalie Gilles Gilbert of the Bruins hurries to the bench enabling the Bruins to add an extra skater in an attempt to take advantage of the delayed penalty. Meanwhile, Ratelle hits Bucyk with a return pass, and the Boston left wing snaps a shot into the net. What is the call?

Solution

The goal is good and the penalty is wiped out because Boston has scored.

SECTION FOUR, RULE 34a and b.

Comment

The calling of penalties in hockey differs from any other game I know, particularly on a delayed call like this one. If you call the penalty as it happens, you'll be penalizing the wrong team. You must wait until the penalized team gains control of the puck before stopping play. This is so much different from, say basketball, where a man may be fouled going in for a shot and the whistle blows immediately. The basket does not count and the man gets one or two free throws. In hockey, if a man is skating in on the net and is fouled in any way, the penalty is not called until the fouled player's team loses control of the puck. And if a goal results, no penalty is assessed at all. This is one of the hardest jobs for a referee to do. It's awfully difficult to hold back blowing that whistle. The normal reaction is to call the penalty as soon as you see it. That's fine for some sports, but not for hockey.

Completing the Play

Problem

Referee Dave Newell has the whistle in his mouth and his arm in the air, signaling a delayed penalty against Philadelphia's Reggie Leach. He won't blow his whistle until the Flyers gain control of the puck. But what constitutes control?

Solution

The rule book is very explicit on this point. The non-offending team must complete its play before the whistle can be blown by Newell.

SECTION FOUR, RULE 34b (*Note* 1).

Comment

"Completion of the play by the non-offending team" means that the puck must come into possession of the team to be penalized—in this case Philadelphia—or that the puck is frozen against the boards by the two teams. It does not mean a rebound off the goalie or accidental contact with the body or equipment of a player on the team to be penalized.

The "Double" Power Play

Problem

Bill Goldsworthy of Minnesota is in the penalty box for holding, giving Atlanta a power play. The Flames apply the pressure, buzzing around the North Stars' goal. Dennis Hextall, trying to kill Goldsworthy's penalty, hooks Eric Vail of the Flames and referee Bruce Hood has his arm in the air to signal another Minnesota penalty. But Atlanta still has possession of the puck, so Hood delays blowing the whistle. Suddenly, Curt Bennett scores for the Flames. What is Hood's call?

Solution

The goal, of course, stands. Hextall's delayed penalty is washed out by the score, and Goldsworthy's penalty is also terminated.

SECTION FOUR, RULE 34 (*Note* 2).

Comment

The rule book interpretation is that Bennett's goal came as a result of Minnesota being shorthanded, and under Rule 27c, a penalized player returns to the ice if a goal is scored against his team while he is in the penalty box. Hextall's delayed penalty is eliminated, just as any delayed penalty would be if a goal is scored against the team committing the infraction before the whistle blows. The fact that the goal came on a power play does not affect Hextall's penalty. The fact that a goal was scored is the key here.

Slow Whistle

Problem

Referee John McCauley signals a holding penalty against Borje Salming of Toronto, who has grabbed Washington's Bill Clement near the Capitals' net. When McCauley raises his arm, he doesn't blow the whistle immediately because Washington has the puck. Goalie Ron Low rushes to the Caps' bench, replaced by an extra skater as Washington tries to move out. But Toronto's checkers have the Caps bottled up in their own end, and even though they are controlling the puck, the Caps are in a jam, especially with the empty net. Suddenly, in a scramble, the puck winds up in Washington's unguarded net. What is the ruling?

Solution

When a team has committed a rules violation calling for a penalty, the whistle is supposed to blow as soon as that team gains control of the puck. As a result, the penalized team cannot score a goal because as soon as it gets the puck, play must end. But if the other team pulls its goalie and then inadvertently puts the puck into its own net, the goal counts. In this example, McCauley must decide whether Washington put the puck in its own net, in which case the goal stands, or whether Toronto put it in, in which case the goal is disallowed.

SECTION FOUR, RULE 34b (*Note* 2).

Comment

The lesson to be learned here is an ounce of prevention is worth a pound of cure. A team lifting its goalie must remember that a goal can still be scored into that empty net by accident and must be careful getting out of its own zone.

Double Penalties

Problem

Philadelphia's Bob Kelly hooks Greg Joly of Washington, and the penalty is signaled by referee Ron Wicks. But the Caps retain control of the puck, so Wicks delays blowing the whistle. Washington rushes an extra skater on the ice after pulling its goalie and closes in on the Flyers' net. Kelly, figuring he's going off the ice anyway, trips Mike Marson of the Caps, and Wicks sees this infraction as well. Still the Caps control, and suddenly Bill Clement of Washington scores. What is Wicks' ruling?

Solution

Clement's goal is good, but Kelly still must go to the penalty box to serve the second of the two infractions Wicks called on him. The goal on the delayed penalty washed out the first infraction, but not the second.

SECTION FOUR, RULE 34c.

Comment

Referees are sometimes hesitant to call double penalties against a single player for two separate infractions. But rules are rules, and if a player commits one, two, or three penalties on the same play, they should be assessed.

Section 5
THE OFFICIALS

Most hockey games are handled by three officials—a referee and two linesmen. Occasionally, two officials will be assigned in amateur and youth games, but that never happens in the professional ranks.

The referee is the man in charge. The linesmen are his helpers. The referee rules on goals and penalties. The linesmen are in charge of icing infractions, offsides violations, and breaking up any altercations that break out in the course of the game.

The thing for the referee to remember is that he is the man in charge of the game—not the players, not the coaches, and not the fans. The referee determines what goes on out there on the ice—no one else.

To be a good referee, a man must set his standard early and stick to it. Hockey players have a way of testing referees early to see just how much they can get away with. You'd be surprised how quickly word spreads around the league that you can get away with such and such with this referee, and you'll get booted for this and that with another.

The rule book is just about as good as the man who is calling the game. In my opinion, when you get on the ice, you can throw the rule book away and referee with common sense. It would be a great substitute and probably an advantage over the rule book. If a referee decided to run a game by the letter of the law as it is set down in the book, he'd have nobody on the ice and fewer people in the stands. Fans come to games to see the players on the ice, not in the penalty box.

No one who has been around the National Hockey League scene for any period of time can deny that the league has come a long way, not only with expansion from 6 teams to 18, but in the operation of the game. When I first broke in as an official, I was a linesman for the old New York Americans. That's right, I said *for* the Americans. In those days, linesmen worked for the home team, not the league, and made their calls with that in mind.

You can understand the problems that hometown officials could cause. And when a linesman came along with the courage to make calls that went against the home team, he usually wound up being fired by the general manager.

All that changed, of course, when hockey decided it would go big league instead of bush league. All officials, from the referee and linesmen to the goal judges and penalty timekeeper, are appointed by the league president.

The Penalty Caller

Problem

During a Montreal attack on Toronto's goal, defenseman Ian Turnbull of the Leafs flagrantly trips the Canadiens' Yvan Cournoyer. The violation takes place behind referee Bob Meyers and there is no call. When play stops, Canadiens' coach Scotty Bowman screams at Meyers, saying everybody in the building saw the violation. "Ask the linesman," yells Bowman.

Solution

Sorry, Scotty, but in hockey, the only man who calls penalties is the referee, and that's the way I think it should be. No two men in the world think alike at the same time.

SECTION FIVE, RULE 36f.

Comment

If the responsibility for the running of the hockey game should be on anyone's shoulder, it should be a single person and not more than one. I'd rather have a referee call a bad

game and call it bad for both sides than two referees, one referee-
eeing badly and the other refereeing well.

Awarding Goals and Assists

Problem

On a scramble in front of Detroit's net, the Rangers score a
goal. Referee Wally Harris reports the goal to the scorer's
bench, saying, "White goal, seven from twelve and eight." But
the goal is announced as Phil Esposito, No. 12, with assists
for No. 7, Rod Gilbert, and No. 8, Steve Vickers.

Solution

This is one part of the game where the referee's opinion
takes a back seat. The awarding of goals and assists is not his
job. That's the scorer's responsibility. The referee reports his
version only to help the scorer.

SECTION FIVE, RULE 36g; SECTION SIX, RULE 55.

Comment

Scorers don't call penalties, and referees don't award goals
and assists. Often, after a period, the player given credit for
the goal skates to the scorer's bench to change the credit,
explaining that another player scored it.

Referee Injury

Problem

My good friend, King Clancy, has done just about every-
thing a man could do in the sport of ice hockey. King played,
coached, managed, and even refereed. He was a man for all
jobs although sometimes his performance, like those of every
player, coach, manager, or referee, didn't satisfy all the cus-
tomers. One night, during his officiating days, Clancy incurred the wrath of a lady sitting in the stands. She let him
have it verbally for a while but when that didn't succeed, she
took more positive action. Waiting for the opportune moment

when Clancy was backed against the boards watching the play, the lady removed one of her hat pins and stuck it right where she thought it would do King the most good.

Solution

A referee has the right to order an unruly spectator removed from the arena today but rarely has to invoke that power. It's usually taken care of by the police in the building.

SECTION FIVE, RULE 36j.

Comment

The rule book says that the game should be halted if the referee leaves the ice. Well, Clancy certainly left the ice, but that game wasn't stopped.

Referee "Misadventure"

Problem

When I was a National Hockey League referee, most travel was done by train. One night, I was on my way from Boston to Montreal and our train got caught in a terrible snow storm. We were delayed for hours and I didn't get to the rink until moments before the game was scheduled to start. But I felt as though I was riding in the pocket of the Lord on that train. One of the other passengers was Frank Calder, president of the league. If I was going to be late, he was going to be late too. And I wouldn't have to make up an excuse.

Solution

The rule book says that in the absences of referee and linesmen, the two clubs shall agree on substitute officials. If they can't agree, then a player on the home team acts as referee and a player from the visiting team serves as linesman.

SECTION FIVE, RULE 36k.

Comment

I don't ever remember this rule having to be used. Officials are usually pretty punctual. I had many a misadventure in my sixteen years in the NHL, but I never missed an assignment.

The Linesman

Problem

In the example where Scotty Bowman protested a penalty committed against his club that the referee had not seen, Bowman demanded that the ref, "ask the linesman." Can the referee do that?

Solution

At his discretion, he certainly can. But the linesman must be asked before volunteering information. He is there to aid the referee, not to call the game for him.

SECTION FIVE, RULE 37b and c.

Comment

They are giving the linesmen more duties every year. It used to be that linesmen could only blow the whistle for offsides, icing, or when the puck left the rink. One of the new duties linesmen have now is to blow the whistle when the puck is struck above the height of shoulder of a player. The linesmen now also face off the puck in the corners. That was the referee's job, but I think I was responsible for the change. I designated linesmen to make those face-offs so that I could stand closer to the net and make, what I thought, was a more important decision if and when it arose. In most of my days as a referee, you had hometown linesmen and minor officials, so it was all the more important for the referee to be in position to make any judgment call that could affect the outcome of the game.

Goal Judges

Problem

There is a scramble in front of the Philadelphia net. Sud-

denly, the puck is shot and appears to hit the inside of the net and then fly right back out. It happens so fast that the players continue the action, thinking the puck struck the goalpost. But the red light is on. The Flyers howl in protest, first to referee Lloyd Gilmour, then to the goal judge who signaled the score.

Solution

The goal stands. Deciding when the puck enters the net is the sole responsibility of the goal judge. Referees can rule on a goal's legality, and Gilmour could have ruled "no goal" for any number of reasons. But the goal judge is the guy who determines whether the puck is in the net and completely over the red line or not.

SECTION FIVE, RULE 38.

Comment

Today's goal judges are a different breed—all very competent and capable individuals. But the goal judges years ago used to be ordered by the coaches and managers of the home team to keep their hands off the switch box when the opposing team had the puck and to keep their hands on the box when the home team had the puck. It's amazing the game survived shenanigans like those.

Official Scorer

Problem

Boston is on the attack against Los Angeles. Jean Ratelle carries the puck over the blue line and then drops it off to Brad Park at the point. Now Ratelle cuts for the net. Park shoots, and the puck deflects off Terry O'Reilly's backside and bounces to Ratelle. The Bruins' center flicks the puck past Rogie Vachon for a goal. Ratelle gets credit for the goal, but how about the assists?

Solution

"Boston goal scored by number ten, Jean Ratelle," begins

the public address announcer's report of the goal. "Assisted by number twenty-two, Brad Park, and number twenty-four, Terry O'Reilly." The rules say assists may be awarded to two players on each goal scored. They do not, however, say assists *must* be awarded to two players.

SECTION FIVE, RULE 40.

Comment

The official scorer can be a very popular individual or he can be a villain, depending on the way he awards assists, and how lenient he is in giving assists. In my opinion, there is too much leniency in awarding assists around the National Hockey League. I believe a man should get an assist if he is directly responsible and deliberately gives the puck to a player who scores a goal—not if it bounces off his derriere or if it bounces off his skate and goes to a teammate. This kind of assist is awarded too often.

Section 6
THE PLAYING RULES

Essentially, hockey is a simple game. Five skaters going against each other, trying to put a round, black hunk of rubber behind a sixth player and into a net that measures 6 feet wide by 4 feet high—an area difficult to defend and just as tough to score into.

The action is fast and furious—often non-stop—and, obviously, it must be governed by rules. There are some things you can do and many others you can't do out there on the ice. The permissible things produce excitement and thrills. The no-nos produce penalties.

There are only a few restrictions in the construction of a team's attack. One of the most important is the requirement that a team remain onsides. Simply stated, that means that no pass may travel over two lines and that no skater may precede the puck into the attacking zone.

Offside violations call for a stoppage of play and a face-off, hockey's equivalent of a jump ball. Other violations that call for penalties produce power plays—manpower advantages that can often lead to goals.

In hockey, the biggest selling point is the game's speed. Many rules are designed to protect that speed—to keep the game moving. And if the game is played properly, the fans won't move out of their seats until the final buzzer ending 60 minutes of speed and excitement.

Misconduct Penalties

Problem

In an altercation on the ice, a player charges after referee

Dave Newell and begins berating the official with a stream of language unfit for a family audience. Newell wheels, set to shut off the criticism with the referee's best weapon—10 minutes in the penalty box for misconduct.

Solution

More likely than not, the offender will be gone for misconduct. But sometimes referees seem more tolerant than at other times. It often depends on who the offender is.

SECTION SIX, RULE 42.

Comment

I think it is incumbent upon the referee to know the habits of the players and to know whether or not obscene language is part of the man's vocabulary or whether he means it as a derogatory remark toward the official. The worst thing an official can have is rabbit ears as he waits for a player to call him something other than his first name while meting out a misconduct penalty. In other words, to paraphrase Gilbert and Sullivan, "Let the punishment fit the criminal."

The Rocket

Problem

Montreal's Maurice "Rocket" Richard's most memorable fight occurred in Boston when he traded punches first with the Bruins' Hal Laycoe and then with linesman Cliff Thompson.

Solution

President Clarence Campbell acted decisively, suspending the volatile Richard for the final three games of the regular season and for the entire Stanley Cup Play-offs as well.

SECTION SIX, RULES 42 and 49d.

Comment

Campbell's decision precipitated the infamous Ste. Cath-

erine Street riot when Canadiens' fans ran wild through
downtown Montreal, causing more than $100,000 worth of
damage. Richard was the only one who could calm the faith-
ful Canadien fans. But don't blame Campbell for this sad blot
in the history of hockey. He was merely carrying out the
penalties as they are outlined in the rule book for assaulting
an official and deliberate injury.

Abuse of Officials

Problem

Referee Bruce Hood calls an elbowing penalty on Terry
Harper of the Detroit Red Wings, who is in the corner
battling for the puck with Minnesota's Craig Cameron.
Harper is incensed by Hood's call, especially when he sees no
penalty indicated for Cameron. He turns to the referee and
starts to complain.

Solution

As soon as Harper opens his mouth, he can be socked with
additional penalties, including a misconduct that carries with
it a minor.

SECTION SIX, RULE 42b.

Comment

This is a new rule added in 1975 that gives more teeth to
referees than they've ever had before. There was a time when
players would take the misconduct and the $50 fines they
carry in order to mouth off. Now those misconducts carry automatic minor penalties as well. That means mouthing off can
leave a loudmouth's team shorthanded. Fifty dollars is one
thing. Two minutes of being shorthanded is quite another.

Attempt to Injure

Problem

Philadelphia and Boston are playing what is called in the

trade a "chippy" hockey game—that is one with a lot of holding, hooking, tripping, and other infractions. As usually happens in this type of game, the minor stuff mushrooms into a major fight, and in the midst of the fight, sticks are swung.

Solution

The rule book is very straightforward on this matter. It says, quite simply, that an attempt to injure an opponent calls for a match penalty. The rule also requires that the matter be reported to the league president for whatever further action might be required.

SECTION SIX, RULE 44.

Comment

In my opinion, referees are far too lenient in their calling of attempt-to-injure penalties. I think it's because of the fact that there is a stigma put on a player tagged with that penalty. Many referees seem to feel that the stigma the penalty leaves on the player is more important in this case than the penalty itself. This penalty also calls for a 5-minute shorthanded situation for the offending team.

Board Checking

Problem

Leo Boivin, who played for so many years as an NHL defenseman, owned one of hockey's very best hip checks. Boivin, who had the build of a fireplug, would crouch low, line up an opposing skater, and then let him have it. Boivin must have delivered thousands of those checks in his eighteen NHL seasons. And I'll bet that some of those checks that were called legal were just about identical to some that were called board checking. How does the referee decide?

Solution

The rule book says board checking is a penalty, but the call is a discretionary one for the referee. It can be either a minor or a major, depending on what the NHL rule book calls "the degree of violence."

Comment

It can be no penalty, a minor penalty, or a major penalty when a player goes banging into those boards. A lot of times, the sound created by the impact decides for the referee whether or not he is going to give a boarding penalty. The only time a board check should be called is when a player deliberately checks a man directly into the boards. A board check should not be called if he rides him into the boards legally. A lot of times, this is misinterpreted.

Broken Stick

Problem

Atlanta is attacking the New York Islanders' net and goalie Chico Resch has blocked several drives. Still the Flames press the attack. Eric Vail fires a shot and defenseman Gerry Hart deflects the puck with his stick. As Hart pursues the puck to the corner, referee Wally Harris blows his whistle.

Solution

Vail's shot shattered Hart's stick but the Islander defenseman, caught up in the action, neglected to drop his broken stick. Playing with a broken stick calls for a 2-minute minor penalty.

Comment

This rule places enormous responsibility on the player. Often, in the heat of the game, a player doesn't realize that his stick is broken and he will hold on to it. That's an automatic penalty because a broken stick can cause extensive injury to the player himself, his teammates, or the opposition. The only player allowed to continue playing with a broken stick is the goaltender.

Broken Stick

Goalie's Sticks

Problem

Gary Smith of the Vancouver Canucks breaks his stick stopping a shot by Toronto's Ian Turnbull. Instinctively, Smith throws away the remainder of his wood and prepares to play goal without a stick until the Canucks can get a replacement to him. Defensemen Mike Robitaille hands his stick to Smith as play continues. Now Robitaille is without a stick, but forward John Gould turns his stick over to the defenseman. Are any penalties imposed?

Solution

No, the exchange of sticks between players on the ice is legal, and it's simply good strategy for a team when it faces the dangerous situation of its goalie trying to defend his net with a broken stick or no stick at all.

SECTION SIX, RULE 46.

Comment

These are fairly recent innovations. Coaches realized that it would be more important for a defenseman or goalie to have a stick in his own zone than it would be for a forward to have one. Thus, the pass off has been approved as a legal maneuver, and it can be an important one.

Charging

Problem

Goalie Ken Dryden circles behind his net to cut off a loose puck and keep it from coming out to a Detroit player on the other side of the Montreal ice. Suddenly, Danny Grant of the Red Wings collides with Dryden behind the Canadiens' goal. When referee Ron Wicks calls Grant for a penalty, the Wings protest, claiming Grant's check was legal and that Dryden was fair game once he left his crease area.

Solution

The penalty stands. The rule book is very specific on this, declaring that the goalie is not fair game outside his crease— and the word not is capitalized. Unnecessary contact with the goalie, even outside his crease, calls for a penalty.

SECTION SIX, RULE 47.

Comment

It used to be that charging was defined in the rule book as three or more strides. They've deleted the number, and now

the book calls for a penalty for a player who "runs or jumps into or charges an opponent." Charging can be a major or minor penalty at the referee's discretion.

Cross-checking and Butt-ending

Problem

A hockey stick can be a harmless piece of equipment, no more imposing than shoulder pads or gloves. Or it can be a lethal weapon in the hands of an enraged player. No piece of

equipment can be more dangerous than a stick being used indiscriminately. It is the job of the referee to control how a player uses his stick.

Solution

The rule book gives the referee discretion to call either

major or minor penalties for cross-checking or butt-ending.
Cross-checking is striking an opponent with both hands holding the stick and no part of the stick on the ice. Butt-ending
means just that—thrusting the butt end of a stick at an opponent. Even a butt-end gesture is enough to draw this penalty.
That's how dangerous the maneuver can be.

SECTION SIX, RULE 48.

Comment

Why they have cross-checking and butt-ending linked in the
rule book I can't understand. Cross-checking is one part of
the game, but butt-ending is quite another—a dirty tactic
plain and simple. When I was refereeing and caught anybody
butt-ending, he got as much as I could give him for this particular infraction.

Deliberate Injury

Problem

In an altercation between Philadelphia and Toronto, Dave

Schultz and Dave Williams square off, drop their gloves, and start fighting. As so often happens when two rambunctious heavyweights start fighting, the linesmen let them go for a while. Eventually, they get tangled up, and one of the players, attempting to break out of the clinch, head-butts the other. What is the call?

Solution

Besides the obvious penalties for fighting, the player who used the head-butt should get a match penalty as well. That's an automatic 5-minute shorthand situation, and if an injury is inflicted by the head-butt, the penalty is 10 minutes of short-handed skating.

SECTION SIX, RULE 49e.

Comment

Like butt-ending, the head-butt is one of hockey's most frowned upon violations. You can see that by the penalties assessed a player using that tactic.

Delaying the Game

Problem

The pressure is on in Detroit's end of the rink with goalie Ed Giacomin blocking a series of shots. The Red Wings are unable to clear against St. Louis' tough forechecking. Finally, Giacomin takes matters into his own hands and after stopping another shot, the goalie, appearing to clear the puck, lifts it into the seats along the sideboards. Immediately, referee Lloyd Gilmour lifts his arm and blows his whistle. What is Gilmour's call?

Solution

The call is delay of the game against Giacomin, and it means St. Louis gets a power play for 2 minutes. The penalty would also apply if Giacomin had batted the puck aside after a stoppage of play.

SECTION SIX, RULE 50a and b.

Comment

They are calling this penalty more today than they ever did before, and I think the reason is that the glass partitions protect the public more nowadays. Years ago, when there was no

glass protection at the side of the rink, I think they were concerned legally that if they called a penalty for deliberate shooting of the puck outside the playing area and the player got a penalty for it, they would be legally bound some way or other in case of injury.

The Moving Goalpost

Problem

Here comes Mickey Redmond of the Detroit Red Wings on a breakaway against Toronto goalie Wayne Thomas. It's one-on-one as Redmond sails in on the Maple Leaf net. Suddenly, Thomas, moving with Redmond, displaces the left goalpost and the net swings free. What's the call?

Solution

In a breakaway situation like that, the displaced goalpost calls for a penalty shot. If it were not a breakaway, displacing the goalpost would call for a 2-minute minor penalty.

SECTION SIX, RULE 50c.

Comment

Moving the goalpost was a favorite trick of netminders during hockey's dark ages. Those old-timers had all kinds of tricks up their sleeves, and they kept the referees on their toes.

Elbowing and Kneeing

Problem

When he played in the National Hockey League, Eric Nesterenko's nickname was Mr. Elbows—but not because his elbows were pretty. It was because they were always obvious, especially in the corners of the rink where Nesterenko did his

best work. Referees had to decide on the legality of his elbows.

Solution

Using an elbow or a knee to foul an opponent means 2 minutes in the penalty box for the offending player. Mr. Nesterenko was a frequent visitor to that area of the rink.

SECTION SIX, RULE 51.

Comment

Elbowing, it seems to me, is being called more often today than it ever was before, and with justification. There are an awful lot of players who are all elbows and knees.

Face-offs

Problem

The puck is in Chicago's zone and the Black Hawks successfully break up a California attack by "freezing" the puck —causing a play stoppage by blocking the Seals from advancing the puck and holding the puck against the sideboards.

Solution

This calls for a face-off—hockey's version of the jump ball. The referee faces off the puck following a goal or at the start of a period. Other face-offs are handled by the linesmen. Nowadays, face-offs are handled vertically—that is, the defensive player stands with his back to his goal and the offensive player stands facing the goal he is trying for. In the past, face-offs were held horizontally.

SECTION SIX, RULE 52.

Comment

Face-offs are very important to winning or losing a hockey game. There are some players who know every quirk and idiosyncrasy of the referee or linesman and just what

movements he makes before he faces off the puck. These are the smart ones. These are the good face-off artists like Stan Mikita and Bobby Clarke.

Falling on the Puck

Problem

The pressure is on in Boston's end of the ice with Kansas City pressing the attack. Wilf Paiement fires a shot that is ticketed for the corner of the net, but Gilles Gilbert gets a pad out just in time to block the shot. The puck falls dead in the crease off Gilbert's pad and Gary Doak, trying to relieve the pressure on his goalie, falls on it.

Solution

The proper call here is a penalty shot. No player except the where else on the ice, this infraction calls for a minor penalty. In the goal crease, it's a penalty shot. goalie is allowed to fall on the puck in the goal crease. Any-

SECTION SIX, RULE 53.

Comment

This rule is not enforced strictly enough by the officials.

There is too much allowance given to players falling on the puck, forcing a stoppage of play. A lot of times, the offending player will escape penalty by just shoving the puck under the goalkeeper.

Fisticuffs

Problem
In a hard-hitting game between New York's hockey neigh-

bors, the Rangers and Islanders, a fight begins between centers Wayne Dillon of the Rangers and Bryan Trottier of the Islanders. When peace is restored, both players head for the penalty box. For how long?

Solution

The likely sentence is identical penalties—either 2 minutes apiece for roughing, or 5 minutes apiece for fighting, or a combination of major and minor penalties. The rule book leaves it to the referee's discretion to dole out the penalties.

SECTION SIX, RULE 54.

Comment

I could talk about this rule forever. I think the word discretion should come out. It should be written, "A major penalty shall be imposed by the referee to a player who starts fisticuffs." This will do away with most of your fisticuffs because no team can afford to play shorthanded repeatedly. I also feel that the minor penalty for retaliation should be imposed, no matter how long the fight continues. The player who starts the fight should get the heavier penalties, and although the rule book provides for that, it rarely happens that way.

Goals and Assists

Problem

Scoring a goal is, after all, what hockey is all about. But sometimes, it isn't as straightforward as a 60-foot slap shot by Bobby Hull. Goals can be scored in a variety of ways, and that's why one of the referee's chief responsibilities is to determine the legality of a goal when it enters the net. When is a goal legal, and when isn't it?

Solution

The rule book outlines half a dozen ways that a goal can be scored and just as many tactics that would make an apparent goal illegal. You cannot, for example, kick the puck into the net. You can, however, be credited with a goal if the puck deflects off your skate and into the net. It is the referee's function to determine whether the puck was kicked or simply deflected.

SECTION SIX, RULE 55.

Comment

The awarding of goals has changed considerably over the course of the years. It used to be the only way a goal could be scored was by the stick of an attacking player or off the body or stick of a defending player. Now a goal can be scored in a whole lot of other ways. This has put into the game a lot of bad goals, but it also has taken out a lot of bad arguments created because of this situation. The comical part of being a high scorer today is you can lead the league if you have a large enough derriere.

A "Legal" Goal

Problem

The New York Islanders are on a power play, and Clark Gillies is stationed at the corner of the Boston net with Bruin defenseman Dallas Smith checking him. Bryan Trottier of New York fires a shot just as Smith drives Gillies against the goalpost and partially inside the goal crease. The puck is headed for the same corner and Gillies turns his skate, directing it into the net. What is the ruling?

Solution

No goal. Directing the puck with the skate erases the score. The goal stands if the puck bounces off the skate but is not directed into the net. And Gillies' presence in the goal crease is all right, because he is being held there by a Boston player.

SECTION SIX, RULE 55d.

Comment

The key to this rule is the word "directing." A puck that bounces off a player's body and into the net is a legal goal,

even if the player did not shoot the puck. As long as he did not direct it, the goal stands. I saw an awful lot of high-scoring backsides in my sixteen years in the NHL.

Official "Targets"

Problem

Washington is on the attack against Atlanta. Mike Marson takes a shot that kicks off linesman Willard Norris and sails into the Flames' net behind goalie Phil Myre. The red goal light goes on. What is the referee's call?

Solution

In this rare case of an official being struck by a shot and the puck landing in the net, it is no goal. If Marson's shot had struck another player and not a linesman, the goal would be good.

SECTION SIX, RULE 55e.

Comment

Years ago, every time the puck hit an official, the whistle was blown, causing a tremendous amount of stops in the game. The Rules Committee has done a good job eliminating situations that merely hold up the game. There's nothing worse, I think, than 14,000 fans and two dozen hockey players waiting around for some action.

Gross Misconduct

Problem

Referee Bruce Hood makes a disputed call and starts getting flack from the fans and players. Hood wheels to see the general manager of the team the call went against carrying on next to the bench, shaking his fist, and making all kinds of noise.

Solution

Hood can tag the GM—yes, even the general manager—with a gross misconduct penalty, ordering him to the dressing room for the remainder of the game. The same penalty may be imposed on a player, coach, or trainer as well.

SECTION SIX, RULE 56.

Comment

This rule isn't used very often. But it can make a referee's job very easy. If he sets a standard and sticks to that standard, he might have to give this penalty only once or twice a season. But he will set a standard that the players, coaches, managers, and trainers will quickly learn and go by in dealing with him.

Handling Puck with Hands

Problem

Minnesota is on the attack against Vancouver. The Ca-

nucks' Bob Dailey intercepts the puck and lifts it, apparently out of danger toward center ice. But Bill Goldsworthy of the North Stars reaches high with his hand and bats the puck back into the Canucks' zone to a teammate. What is the call?

Solution

Goldsworthy's tactic is illegal, and the face-off comes outside of the Vancouver blue line. The rule book further specifies that if a player closes his hand on the puck, it calls for a minor penalty. If Goldsworthy had merely knocked the puck down and kept it in play that way, no violation would have been signaled and play could have continued. By swatting it ahead to another North Star player, he caused the whistle and the ensuing face-off.

SECTION SIX, RULE 57.

Comment

The purpose of this rule is to insure continuous action and to penalize players who stop the action by holding the puck or attempt to take advantage of a teammate's position by batting the puck deliberately toward him. Discretion of the referee is very important here. He must use his common sense. It's very tough for a player not to close his hand on the puck that hits him flush in the palm of his glove.

High Sticks

Problem

There is a scramble in front of Buffalo's net with Pittsburgh applying the pressure. Suddenly, a whistle interrupts the action and referee Bryan Lewis points at Pierre Larouche of the Penguins, who is swinging at the puck.

Solution

As an attacking player, Larouche would have no reason to be high-sticking one of the Sabres. But high-sticking is what this penalty is for. The rule book says a player can be assessed a minor penalty if he carries the stick above the

height of his shoulder. Even if this happens accidentally, a referee calling a tight game could catch it.

SECTION SIX, RULE 58a.

Comment
The rule that applies says a penalty may be imposed at the discretion of the referee. I don't ever remember a penalty

being imposed on anybody for just carrying the stick above the height of the shoulder. The penalty usually is given for using the stick in some way, either to swat the puck or to swat an opponent.

High-sticking Injury

Problem

Most fans know that if a player cuts an opponent with his stick and draws blood, he is assessed a 5-minute major penalty during which he must remain off the ice for the full term, no matter how many goals are scored. But what if he strikes an opponent with a high stick and doesn't draw blood?

Solution

The same penalty applies. The rule book says nothing about blood in that situation. All it says is that if a high stick causes injury to the head or face of an opponent, the major penalty should be called.

SECTION SIX, RULE 58c.

Comment

This rule has always been controversial because of the fact that it is commonly known in hockey that drawing blood from an opponent automatically calls for a 5-minute penalty. But actually what the rule says is that injury to the face or head is enough cause for the 5-minute penalty to be imposed. Remember, the rule says injury, so you do not have to draw blood to receive a major penalty.

Holding

Problem

The attacking St. Louis Blues zoom into Pittsburgh's end of the ice. Trailing the play is Blues' winger Pierre Plante. As Garry Unger spots Plante coming over the blue line, he shovels the puck to the winger. But Plante never reaches the pass. Defenseman Ron Stackhouse has grabbed his jersey, halting his progress. Referee Bob Meyers blows his whistle. What is the call?

Solution

Stackhouse goes to the penalty box for 2 minutes for holding. This is a favorite tactic of a team trying to disrupt an attack or slow up an opponent. But the referee must use common sense when calling it. He must set a standard and stick to it. He may let a casual grab get by, but if he does that for one team, he must do the same for the other. He must determine how flagrant the hold must be for him to blow the whistle and then stick to that yardstick.

SECTION SIX, RULE 59.

Comment

This is one of hockey's most common penalties. It should be interpreted just as the rule book states it: "A minor penalty shall be imposed on a player who holds a player with hands or stick or in any other way." Some hockey players are excellent in this area. The old Toronto Maple Leafs were the best team in the league at holding.

Who's Holding?

Problem

I was the referee for a game involving the Detroit Red Wings and Chicago Black Hawks. The two teams were going at each other pretty good all night long, and midway through the third period Chicago's Johnny Mariucci collided with Black Jack Stewart of the Red Wings. Both players lost their sticks in the crash, and when they recovered, both went looking for their sticks. Unfortunately, both saw the same one and grabbed it. Neither would let go, and finally I had to blow my whistle. Someone was holding, but which one was it?

Solution

Hockey players identify their sticks by printing their uniform numbers on the knob. So I looked at the stick. When I found Stewart's number, that meant he was entitled to the stick and Mariucci was holding. That cost John 2 minutes in the penalty box.

SECTION SIX, RULE 59.

Comment

Wouldn't it be nice if every referee's dilemma were as easy to solve as that one?

Hooking

Problem

St. Louis is on the attack in the Rangers' end of the ice and Gary Unger carries the puck over the blue line. Defenseman Ron Greschner, pursuing Unger, catches the Blues' center around the midsection with his stick. What is the call?

Solution

Greschner should go for hooking—a 2-minute minor penalty. If Unger did not have the puck, the penalty could be called interference instead.

SECTION SIX, RULE 60.

Comment

This penalty is not called nearly enough. If referees called hooking more often, the game would open up and it would be more enjoyable for the spectators. Hooking usually occurs when a less-talented hockey player is trying to slow up one of the better skaters.

Icing the Puck

Problem

Buffalo is attacking Montreal goalie Ken Dryden. The Canadiens' netminder makes three tough saves before Serge Savard recovers the puck and lofts it down ice to relieve the pressure. The puck coasts to the other end of the rink where it is recovered by Buffalo defenseman Jim Schoenfeld, who takes his time going back for the puck. He looks for the icing call. But linesman Leon Stickles waves it off. Why?

Solution

Icing the puck to terminate an opponent's attack is a legitimate defensive maneuver that ordinarily results in a face-off deep in the zone of the team committing the infraction. But there are several reasons why the icing call can be eliminated.

One is if a defending player has a chance to play the puck before it passes his goal line. Another is if the puck deflects off one of the opposing team's players on its way down ice.

SECTION SIX, RULE 61.

Comment

If the icing rule is interpreted and called properly, it can keep a hockey game moving along at a rapid pace. The linesman has to make sure that the defending player on the icing rule attempts to play the puck. Many linesmen are too lax on this and call the icing almost automatically, subsequently stopping the game. Icing, of course, is never called against a team that is playing shorthanded.

Staying in the Penalty Box

Problem

Jim McKenny is in the penalty box for Toronto after elbowing California goalie Gilles Meloche. McKenny's sentence is 2 minutes, and the Maple Leafs successfully kill off the time. With about 5 seconds left in the penalty, Lanny McDonald lifts the puck the length of the ice, ending California's last power-play try. But as his penalty expires, McKenny remains in the penalty box, waiting for a Seal player to pick up the puck. He's being cagy, delaying his exit from the penalty box so that the Leafs will technically still be shorthanded when California recovers the puck. That would eliminate the icing call and prevent the face-off from being held deep in Toronto's end of the ice.

Solution

The icing stands. It is determined not by what McKenny does and whether or not he goes back on the ice when he should, but by the clock. As soon as the penalty is over, the teams are considered to be equal in manpower, and both are prone to icing calls.

SECTION SIX, RULE 61a.

Comment

This is just a smart play by McKenny, who might get away with it if the linesman, who is responsible for icing calls, isn't alert. This often calls for split-second judgment by the linesman, who must know exactly when the penalty is over to call it properly.

Interference

Problem

Interference is the most prevalent violation in hockey. The referee's job, as in all violations, is to determine when it has occurred and when the contact is justified. Suppose, for example, Gil Perreault of the Sabres carries the puck into California's zone. He passes off to Rene Robert and then heads for the net. There he is met by the Seals' Dave Hrechkosy. Can referee Dave Newell call Hrechkosy for interference?

Solution

It depends on when Hrechkosy makes contact with Perreault and how tight a game Newell is calling. Technically, a man may be checked while carrying the puck or immediately after passing it. If, however, Robert has already relayed Perreault's pass to another Sabre, then Hrechkosy's contact with Perreault could be called interference.

SECTION SIX, RULE 62a.

Comment

This is a rule that must take more discretion and common sense than any other in the book. Basically, the rule means you may not impede the progress of any player not last in possession of the puck. If this rule was enforced as it is written, you would have two or three penalties every time the puck is carried down the ice. A lot of penalties are called by other names, but technically unless a man is in possession of the puck when he is fouled, the call should be interference. Numerous times you will hear calls for holding, tripping, high-

sticking, etc. But technically, the term should be interference unless the man was last in possession of the puck when fouled.

Interference by a Spectator

Problem

In a scramble for the puck near the boards, Montreal's

Yvan Cournoyer is checked hard by Bobby Orr of Boston. Cournoyer's body is pinned against the boards and his stick is extended over the glass partition. A fan grabs the stick of the Canadien forward. What is the call?

Solution

The referee must blow his whistle to stop play, unless the Canadiens retain control of the puck. In this case, it's very much like a delayed penalty where the ref does not blow his whistle until the offending team gains control of the puck.

SECTION SIX, RULE 63a.

Comment

This is another rule requiring discretion and common sense. You certainly aren't going to stop the play and take a scoring chance away from the hockey club because a spectator is interfering with the offensive player. If the fans are interfering with a defensive player who had a chance to get into the action, then the whistle should be blown.

Kicking a Player

Problem

In the final round of a play-off series one year, two players got involved in a center ice collision and fell to the ice in a tangle. Play continued without them and as one of the players attempted to get to his feet, in his anxiety he kicked out with his skate. He made no contact with the other player, and it was uncertain whether any was intended. What should the referee's call have been?

Solution

A player caught kicking at another gets an automatic match penalty. Contact doesn't matter. Even a kicking motion is enough to draw the sentence. A suspension from future games can be tacked on as well.

SECTION SIX, RULE 64.

Comment

The penalty is certainly not strong enough in my opinion. It should be more than a match penalty. I think it should involve a mandatory suspension because kicking is the worst act a player can take against another player. But if he is penalized for a kick, his reputation will go around the league, and I don't think he'll kick again.

Kicking the Puck

Problem

Center Derek Sanderson of the St. Louis Blues has lost his stick while play continues in the Blues' end of the ice. Pittsburgh is pressing the attack and Sanderson has no chance to recover his stick or skate to the bench for a replacement. Suddenly, the puck comes to him, and the Blues' player kicks it to a teammate. What is the call?

Solution

There is no whistle and play continues. Sanderson has done nothing illegal. Kicking the puck is a perfectly acceptable and proper tactic for a player who has lost his stick, or even one who has his stick but can't get it into position quickly enough to play the puck.

SECTION SIX, RULE 65.

Comment

Some players are very adept at kicking the puck. Red Kelly, who starred for so many years with Detroit and Toronto, was one of the best in the business at that maneuver. He could stickhandle with his skates better than anybody in the league when he was playing. A lot of fans don't understand that not only are you allowed to kick the puck, but you could play the game without a stick if you so desire.

Leaving the Bench

Problem

Philadelphia's Bob Kelly is in the penalty box serving a minor for holding. Suddenly an altercation breaks out on the ice between the Flyers and Minnesota North Stars. As the players pair off, Kelly leaves the penalty box to join in the brawl. What price must he pay for his involvement?

Solution

Besides his original penalty and whatever he gets for the fight, Kelly draws a double minor and game misconduct for leaving the penalty box. The penalty would be the same if he had left the players' bench instead of the penalty box.

SECTION SIX, RULE 66a and b.

Comment

This rule is instrumental in cutting down brawls. It's quite a drastic penalty. A double minor means giving the other team a manpower advantage for 4 minutes and puts your club in a very precarious position. Sometimes, it is difficult for the referee to determine which player has left the players' bench or the penalty box first. If he has any doubt, he may consult the linesmen or minor officials. I always felt it was a good idea to talk with the linesmen many times during a game. While he may not call a penalty, he can certainly help you when you're in doubt.

Off the Bench and Out of the Game

Problem

The Philadelphia Flyers and Pittsburgh Penguins got into a bench-clearing brawl with players from both teams charging on to the ice to get into the battle. The first player off the Flyers' bench was rookie defenseman Jack McIlhargey—the second time inside of a couple of weeks that he had had that dubious distinction. What happens to the young man?

Solution

For starters, he gets a double minor penalty and a game misconduct for being the first player to leave the bench. His second violation of the rule also earns him a 1-game suspension.

SECTION SIX, RULE 66b and e.

Comment

Mr. McIlhargey will have to learn to stay on the bench when those brawls break out. Otherwise, he's going to be sitting out more games than he plays because every time he leaves the bench, he'll get additional game suspensions.

Molesting Officials

Problem

A few years ago during a Stanley Cup Play-off game, Bobby Orr of the Bruins was assessed with a penalty by referee John Ashley. Orr went slightly wild over the call and charged Ashley.

Solution

That was the last thing Orr did on the ice that night. Ashley tagged him with a game misconduct penalty as soon as he made contact with the official. That's called molesting an official, and it's a hockey no-no.

SECTION SIX, RULE 67.

Comment

This is certainly one of my favorite rules in the book. If a referee commands the respect of the hockey players in the league in which he is working, this should never, never happen. In all of my years in the NHL, it never happened to me. But many referees and/or linesmen have been attacked by players, making this rule necessary.

Obscene or Profane Language or Gestures

Problem

Someone once wrote that a picture is worth a thousand words. So, sometimes, is a gesture. Suppose a hockey player gets angry at a call. Instead of mouthing off to the referee, he gives him one of a number of universally recognized gestures —perhaps the hands on the throat signifying choke. What can the referee do?

Solution

The answer is plenty. Just as oral abuse can rate a misconduct penalty, so, too, can a gesture. If it happens in the vicinity of the players' bench, a bench minor penalty resulting in a power play for the other team may be imposed.

SECTION SIX, RULE 68.

Comment

Gestures always annoyed me very much, and I gave as much as I could for a gesture. Obscene or profane language is a discretionary decision to be made by the referee, who must decide whether the player involved is using his normal vocabulary or reaching out for some special words to express his anger. If a player cusses a referee privately, that's one thing. If he does it where he can be overheard by half a dozen other players, you have no alternative but to penalize him in order to maintain respect from the other players.

Offsides

Problem

Here come the Islanders on a rush up ice. Center Jude Drouin is carrying the puck with Eddie Westfall and J. P. Parise on the wings. As the trio hits the attacking blue line, Westfall and Parise pull up, trying to stay onsides. However, linesman Ray Scampinelo whistles the play down. What went wrong?

Solution

One of the Islanders went over the blue line before Drouin and the puck got there. That's offsides and calls for a face-off outside the blue line. A skater is considered offsides if both

his skates are over the blue line before the puck. He is onsides if he has one skate straddling the blue line. That's why you see skaters sometimes looking as though they are walking a tightrope at that blue line.

SECTION SIX, RULES 69 and 71.

Comment

The offsides rule is easy to understand. Just remember that no player on the attacking team can precede the puck into the attacking zone. And the important thing is that the determining factor for offsides is the position of both skates in relation to the blue line. The key word here is both. One skate over the blue line ahead of the puck does not throw a player offsides.

Two-line Passes

Problem

Montreal's Yvan Cournoyer, one of the fleetest skaters in the NHL, is hanging in the neutral zone while Washington attacks the Canadiens' end of the ice. Suddenly, Jacques Lemaire intercepts a pass and spots Cournoyer out near the center red line. Lemaire relays a slick pass and Cournoyer is off and running with the puck. Is the pass legal?

Solution

As long as Lemaire's pass does not go over two lines before Cournoyer gets it, the play is legitimate. A two-line pass causes an offsides call.

SECTION SIX, RULE 70.

Comment

Cournoyer must have scored dozens of goals this way. His

speed makes him impossible to catch, and as long as he receives the pass-out on Montreal's side of the center red line,
the play is onsides.

Clearing the Zone

Problem

Los Angeles is on the attack with five skaters inside the
Toronto blue line. Suddenly, the puck gets past point man
Butch Goring and slides back into the neutral zone. Goring
recovers it quickly and returns it to the Leafs' end, but linesman Claude Bechard whistles the play down. What went
wrong?

Solution

When the puck left the Leafs' zone, the L.A. skaters had to
clear the zone as well. If Goring sent the puck back into
Toronto's end before all the Los Angeles skaters were out of
the zone, the Kings were guilty of offsides.

SECTION SIX, RULE 71.

Comment

Really, this form of offsides is another version of preceding
the puck into the attacking zone. When the puck leaves the
attacking zone, so must the attacking players. Otherwise, if
they stay, they will have been there before the puck when it is
returned.

Playable Puck

Problem

Suppose Boston is clearing the puck out of its own end of
the ice. Defenseman Brad Park lifts the puck against the sideboards, and in its flight, the rubber lands on the ledge of the
boards. Does that cause the referee or linesman to blow the
whistle?

Solution

No. The puck is considered to be still in play and may be knocked back to the ice surface by any skater's hand or stick.

SECTION SIX, RULES 72d and 73a.

Comment

The idea in hockey is to keep moving. There are penalties for deliberately delaying the game. Where officials can avoid blowing the whistle and halting the action, they will. That's why the rule book is specific about this unusual occurrence. Keeping the game in motion is what an official's first concern should be.

Puck in Motion

Problem

Kansas City gains possession of the puck after breaking up a Minnesota attack. Guy Charron has it behind the Scouts' net and is getting ready to start out with it. In front of the net, forechecking for Minnesota, are Dennis Hextall and Norm Gratton. Charron is bottled up and can't get out. So he stops, waiting behind the net for Minnesota to let up the pressure. Referee Wally Harris blows his whistle. What is the call?

Solution

The first time it happens, Harris orders a face-off with the Scouts forced to surrender the puck because Charron was not advancing it. The second time it happens, Harris can impose a minor penalty.

SECTION SIX, RULE 73.

Comment

Hockey is the fastest game in the world, and to maintain its speed and excitement, the puck must be kept in motion.

Out of Sight, Out of Play

Problem

There is a scramble in front of Pittsburgh's net as St. Louis

presses the attack. Just as Red Berenson apparently slips the puck behind goalie Michel Plasse, the whistle blows. Referee Ron Wicks is waving the goal off. What went wrong?

Solution

It's no goal because referee Wicks lost sight of the puck. The rule book says that as soon as the referee cannot see the puck, he must blow the play dead and a face-off is held.

SECTION SIX, RULE 74.

Comment

Sometimes the referee places himself in a position where he can't see the puck. He must use his own good sense here and not blow the play dead when he's the only one in the arena who can't see the puck.

Puck Striking Official

Problem

Montreal is on the attack and setting up in Vancouver's end of the ice. Steve Shutt shovels a pass to Pete Mahovlich, and Mahovlich spots Guy Lafleur busting down the right side. Mahovlich relays the puck, but before it gets to Lafleur, it strikes linesman John D'Amico. What happens?

Solution

Play continues. An official is considered part of the rink like the board or the goalposts.

SECTION SIX, RULE 75.

Comment

Usually, hockey officials stay out of the way of the puck pretty well. I've climbed a few sideboards to avoid getting hit by it. But occasionally, it can't be helped. In this case, it might cost Montreal a scoring chance. But the next time it happens to the Canadiens, the puck might deflect to a player who would not otherwise have had a decent shot at the net.

These things all have a way of balancing themselves out in the long run.

Slashing

Slashing

Problem

Defenseman Dave Burrows of Pittsburgh collides with Dan Maloney of Detroit. As the two players regain their feet, no penalty has been called. But Maloney, angered by the crash, makes a slashing motion with his stick at Burrows, as much a warning as a threat. Immediately, referee John McCauley blows his whistle.

Solution

Maloney goes off for slashing, even if he makes no contact with Burrows. Intent is enough, and McCauley can send him off for a minor or major penalty, at the referee's discretion.

SECTION SIX, RULE 77.

Comment

A gesture is enough to make a player liable to a slashing penalty, and I think that's a good thing. I also think this penalty should be called more often than it is.

Spearing

Problem

When Doug Harvey was an outstanding defenseman with the Montreal Canadiens, he had quite a feud with Red Sullivan of the New York Rangers. Harvey accused Sully of kicking skates, one of the tactics hockey players frown upon. Harvey warned his adversary to stop, and when that didn't work harvey took the law into his own hands, spearing Sullivan with the blade of his stick.

Solution

Spearing today calls for an automatic major penalty because of the dangerous nature of the action. Following the Harvey incident, Sullivan underwent emergency surgery and his spleen was removed. He received the last rites on the operating table, but pulled through.

SECTION SIX, RULE 78.

Comment

This is a difficult penalty for the referee to catch always. A spear can be delivered subtly. But like butt-ending and kicking, if you get the reputation of spearing, you won't last long in this game.

Tripping

Problem

Montreal's Guy Lafleur is skating with the puck in Toronto's zone. Rod Seiling of the Maple Leafs is checking the speedy Canadien and gets the puck away. As he does, Lafleur tumbles to the ice and looks to referee Bruce Hood for a tripping call. He does not, however, get it. Why?

Solution

The rule book calls for a minor tripping penalty imposed against any player who places his stick, knee, foot, arm, hand, or elbow in such a manner that it shall cause an opponent to trip. But it also says that if, in the opinion of the referee, the

trip occurs when a player is unquestionably hook-checking
the puck and obtains possession, no tripping is called.

SECTION SIX, RULE 83.

Comment

You do not give a player a penalty for tripping if the opposing player steps on his stick and falls down. And you do
not give a tripping penalty if the player doing the tripping is
checking the puck away from an opponent.

Appendix I
OFFICIALS' SIGNALS

INTERFERENCE

Crossed arms stationary in front of chest.

CROSS-CHECKING

A forward and backward motion with both fists clenched extending from the chest.

ICING

Arms folded across the chest. When the puck is shot or deflected in such a manner as to produce a possible icing of the puck the rear linesman will signal to his partner by raising either arm over his head (same as in Slow Whistle). Immediately the conditions required to establish "icing the puck" have occurred, the forward linesman will respond with the same Slow Whistle signal and the rear linesman will blow his whistle to stop the play and both will give the proper "icing" signal.

CHARGING

Rotating clenched fists around one another in front of chest.

SLASHING

A chopping motion with edge of one hand across the opposite forearm

DELAYED CALLING OF PENALTY

Referee extends arm and points once to penalized player.

ELBOWING

Tapping either elbow with the opposite hand.

HOLDING

Clasping the wrist of the whistle hand well in front of the chest.

HOOKING

A tugging motion with both arms, as if pulling something toward the stomach.

BOARDING

Pounding the closed fist of one hand into the open palm of the other hand.

HIGH-STICKING

Holding both fists, clenched, one immediately above the other, at the height of the forehead.

TRIPPING

Strike the right leg with the right hand below the knee keeping both skates on the ice.

"WASH-OUT"

Both arms swung laterally across the body with palms down:
1. When used by the referee it means goal disallowed.
2. When used by linesmen it means there is no icing or no off-side.

ROUGHING, FIGHTING

A "punching" motion with the arm extending from the side.

MISCONDUCT

Placing of both hands on hips and pointing to penalized player.

SLOW WHISTLE

Arm, in which whistle is not held, extended above head. If play returns to neutral zone without stoppage, arm is drawn down the instant the puck crosses the line.

Appendix II
OFFICIAL NHL RULES

SECTION ONE—THE RINK

Rule 1. Rink

The game of "Ice Hockey" shall be played on an ice surface known as a "RINK."

Rule 2. Dimensions of Rink

(a) The official size of the rink shall be two hundred feet long and eighty-five feet wide. The corners shall be rounded in the arc of a circle with radius of twenty-eight feet.

The rink shall be surrounded by a wooden wall or fence known as the "boards" which shall extend not less than forty inches and not more than forty-eight inches above the level of the ice surface. The ideal height of the boards above the ice surface shall be forty-two inches. Except for the official markings provided for in these rules the entire playing surface and the boards shall be white in colour except the kick plate at the bottom of the boards which shall be light blue or light yellow in colour.

Any variations from any of the foregoing dimensions shall require official authorization by the League.

(b) The boards shall be constructed in such manner that the surface facing the ice shall be smooth and free of any obstruction or any object that could cause injury to players.

All doors giving access to the playing surface must swing away from the ice surface.

All glass, wire or other types of protective screens and gear used to hold them in position shall be mounted on the boards on the side away from the playing surface.

Rule 3.   **Goal Posts and Nets**

(a)   Ten feet from each end of the rink and in the center of a red line two inches wide, drawn completely across the width of the ice and continued vertically up the side of the boards, regulation goal posts and nets shall be set in such manner as to remain stationary during the progress of a game. The goal posts shall be kept in position by means of metal rods or pipes affixed in the ice or floor and projecting a minimum of eight inches above the ice surface.

     Where the length of the playing surface exceeds two hundred feet the goal line and goal posts may be placed not more than fifteen feet from the end of the rink.

(b)   The goal posts shall be of approved design and material, extending vertically four feet above the surface of the ice and set six feet apart measured from the inside of the posts. A cross bar of the same material as the goal posts shall extend from the top of one post to the top of the other.

     (NOTE) *For League games the "NHL Official Goal Frame and Net" are approved and adopted. The design and specifications set out in the Plan of Goal printed in this Rule Book are official.*

(c)   There shall be attached to each goal frame a net of approved design made of white nylon cord which shall be draped in such a manner as to prevent the puck coming to rest on the outside of it.

     A skirt of heavy white nylon fabric or heavyweight white canvas shall be laced around the "3" base plate of the goal frame in such a way as to protect the net from being cut or broken. This skirt shall not project more than one inch above the base plate.

     (NOTE) *The frame of the goal including the small "3" attached to the top cross bar shall be draped with a nylon mesh net so as to completely enclose the back of the frame. The net shall be made of three-ply twisted twine (0.130 inch diameter) or equivalent braided twine of multifilament white nylon with an approximate tensile Strength of 700 pounds. The size of the mesh shall be two and one-half inches (inside measurement) from each knot to each diagonal knot when fully stretched. Knotting shall be made so as to ensure no sliding of the twine. The net shall be laced to the frame with medium white nylon cord no smaller in size than ♯ 21.*

(d)   The goal posts, cross bar and the exterior surface of other supporting framework for the goal shall be painted entirely in red. The surface of the base plate inside the goal and supports other than the goal posts shall be painted white.

(e) The red line, two inches wide, between the goal posts on the ice and extended completely across the rink, shall be known as the "GOAL LINE."

(f) The Goal area, enclosed by the goal line and the base of the goal, shall be painted white.

Rule 4. Goal Crease

(a) In front of each goal a "GOAL CREASE" area shall be marked by a red line two inches in width.

(b) The goal crease shall be laid out as follows: One foot from the outside of each goal post, lines four feet in length and two inches in width shall be drawn at right angles to the goal line and the points of these lines farthest from the goal line shall be joined by another line, two inches in width.

(c) The goal crease area shall include all the space outlined by the crease lines and extending vertically four feet to the level of the top of the goal frame.

Rule 5. Division of Ice Surface

(a) The ice area between the two goals shall be divided into three parts by lines, twelve inches in width, and blue in colour, drawn sixty feet out from the goal lines, and extended completely across the rink, parallel with the goal lines, and continued vertically up the side of boards.

(b) That portion of the ice surface in which the goal is situated shall be called the "DEFENDING ZONE" of the team defending that goal; the central portion shall be known as the "NEUTRAL ZONE," and the portion farthest from the defended goal as the "ATTACKING ZONE."

(c) There shall also be a line, twelve inches in width, and red in colour, drawn completely across the rink in center ice, parallel with the goal lines and continued vertically up the side of the boards, known as the "CENTER LINE." This line shall contain at regular intervals markings of a uniform distinctive design which will easily distinguish it from the two blue lines . . . the outer edges of which must be continuous.

Rule 6. Center Ice Spot and Circle

A circular blue spot, twelve inches in diameter, shall be marked exactly in the center of the rink; and with this spot as a center a circle of fifteen feet radius shall be marked with a blue line two inches in width.

Rule 7.   Face-off Spots in Neutral Zone

Two red spots two feet in diameter shall be marked on the ice in the Neutral Zone five feet from each blue line. The spots shall be forty-four feet apart and each shall be a uniform distance from the adjacent boards.

Rule 8.   End Zone Face-off Spots and Circles

(a) In both End Zones and on both sides of each goal, red face-off spots and circles shall be marked on the ice. The face-off spots shall be two feet in diameter and the circles shall be two inches wide with a radius of fifteen feet from the center of the face-off spots. Twenty feet from the goal line and parallel to it red lines two feet in length and two inches wide shall be marked on the ice extending from the outer edge of both sides of each face-off circle.

Parallel to the goal line and equidistant from and on opposite sides of the center of each end face-off spot two red lines three feet in length and three inches in width and six feet apart shall be marked on the ice. Perpendicular from the center of these lines and extending away from the center face-off circle is drawn a line six feet long and three inches wide. (The effect of these lines is to produce a "T" on opposite sides of the center face-off spot.)

In addition, there shall be a line six inches long and two inches wide extending out from the "12 o'clock" and "6 o'clock" positions of the face-off spots.

(b) The location of the face-off spots shall be fixed in the following manner:

Along a line twenty feet from each goal line and parallel to it, mark two points twenty-two feet on both sides of the straight line joining the centers of the two goals. Each such point shall be the center of a face-off spot and circle.

Rule 9.   Players' Bench

(a) Each rink shall be provided with seats or benches for the use of players of both teams and the accommodations provided including benches and doors shall be uniform for both teams. Such seats or benches shall have accommodation for at least fourteen persons of each team, and shall be placed immediately alongside the ice, in the Neutral Zone, as near to the center of the rink as possible with doors opening in the Neutral Zone and convenient to the dressing rooms.

The players' benches should be on the same side of the playing surface opposite the penalty bench and should be separated by a substantial distance. Each players' bench should be twenty-four feet in length.

Where physically possible each players' bench shall have two doors opening in the Neutral Zone and all doors opening to the playing surface shall be constructed so that they swing inward.

(b) None but players in uniform, Manager, Coach and Trainer shall be permitted to occupy the benches so provided.

Rule 10. Penalty Bench

(a) Each rink must be provided with benches or seats to be known as the "PENALTY BENCH." These benches or seats must be capable of accommodating a total of ten persons including the Penalty Timekeepers. Separate penalty benches shall be provided for each team and they shall be situated on opposite sides of the Timekeeper's area. The penalty bench(es) must be situated opposite the Neutral Zone.

(b) On the ice immediately in front of the Penalty Timekeeper's seat there shall be marked in red on the ice a semi-circle of ten feet radius and two inches in width which shall be known as the "REFEREE'S CREASE."

Rule 11. Signal and Timing Devices

(a) Each rink must be provided with a gong, or other suitable sound device, for the use of Timekeepers.

(b) Each rink shall be provided with some form of electrical clock for the purpose of keeping the spectators, players and game officials accurately informed as to all time elements at all stages of the game including the time remaining to be played in any period and the time remaining to be served by at least five penalized players on each team.

Time recording for both game time and penalty time shall show time remaining to be played or served.

(c) Behind each goal electric lights shall be set up for the use of the Goal Judges. A red light will signify the scoring of a goal. Where automatic lights are available, a green light will signify the end of a period or a game.

(NOTE) *A goal cannot be scored when a green light is showing.*

Rule 12.   **Police Protection**

All clubs shall provide adequate police or other protection for all players and officials at all times.

The Referee shall report to the President any failure of this protection observed by him or reported to him with particulars of such failure.

SECTION TWO—TEAMS

Rule 13.   **Composition of Team**

(a) A team shall be composed of six players, who shall be under contract to the club they represent.

(b) Each player and each goalkeeper listed in the line-up of each team shall wear an individual identifying number at least ten inches high on the back of his sweater.

All players of each team shall be dressed uniformly in conformity with approved design and colour of their helmets, sweaters, pants, stockings and boots. Any player or goalkeeper not complying with this provision shall not be permitted to participate in the game.

Each member club shall design and wear distinctive and contrasting uniforms for their home and road games, no parts of which shall be interchangeable except the pants.

Rule 14.   **Captain of Team**

(a) One Captain shall be appointed by each team, and he alone shall have the privilege of discussing with the Referee any questions relating to interpretation of rules which may arise during the progress of a game. He shall wear the letter "C," approximately three inches in height and in contrasting color, in a conspicuous position on the front of his sweater.

(b) The Referee and Official Scorer shall be advised prior to the start of each game, the name of the Captain of the team and the designated substitute.

(c) No goalkeepers shall be entitled to exercise the privilege of Captain.

(d) Only the Captain, when invited to do so by the Referee, shall have the privilege of discussing any point relating to the interpretation of rules. Any Captain or player who comes off the bench and makes any protest or intervention with the Officials for any purpose must be assessed a misconduct penalty.

A complaint about a penalty is NOT a matter "relating to the interpretation of the rules" and a misconduct penalty shall be imposed against any Captain or other player making such a complaint.

(e) No playing Coach or playing Manager shall be permitted to act as Captain.

Rule 15.   **Players in Uniform**

(a) At the beginning of each game the Manager or Coach of each team shall list the players and goalkeepers who shall be eligible to play in the game. Not more than seventeen players, exclusive of goalkeepers, shall be permitted.

In play-offs seventeen players, exclusive of goalkeepers, shall be permitted.

(b) A list of names and numbers of all eligible players and goalkeepers must be handed to the Referee or Official Scorer before the game, and no change shall be permitted in the list or addition thereto shall be permitted after the commencement of the game.

(c) Each team shall be allowed one goalkeeper on the ice at one time. The goalkeeper may be removed and another "player" substituted. Such substitute shall not be permitted the privileges of the goalkeeper.

(d) Each team shall have on its bench, or on a chair immediately beside the bench, a substitute goalkeeper who shall at all times be fully dressed and equipped ready to play.

When the substitute goalkeeper enters the game he will take his position without delay and no warm-up shall be permitted.

(e) Except when both goalkeepers are incapacitated, no player on the playing roster in that game shall be permitted to wear the equipment of the goalkeeper.

(f) In League Play-off games if both listed goalkeepers are incapacitated, that team shall be entitled to dress and play any available goalkeeper who is eligible. No delay shall be permitted in taking his position in the goal, and he shall be permitted the two-minute warm-up.

(g) The Referee shall report to the President for disciplinary action any delay in making a substitution of goalkeepers.

Rule 16.   **Starting Line-Up**

(a) Prior to the start of the game, at the request of the Referee, the Manager or Coach of the visiting team is required to name the starting line-up to the Referee or the Official Scorer. At any time in the game at the request of the Referee, made to the Captain or Alternate Captain, the visiting team must place a playing line-up on the ice and promptly commence play.

(b) Prior to the start of the game the Manager or Coach of the home team, having been advised by the Official Scorer or the Referee the names of the starting line-up of the visiting team, shall name the starting line-up of the home team which information shall be conveyed by the Official Scorer or the Referee to the Coach of the visiting team.

(c) No change in the starting line-up of either team as given to the Referee or Official Scorer, or in the playing line-up on the ice, shall be made until the game is actually in progress. For an infraction of this rule a bench minor penalty shall be imposed upon the offending team, provided such infraction is called to the attention of the Referee before the second face-off in the first period takes place.

(d) Following the stoppage of play the visiting team shall promptly place a line-up on the ice ready for play and no substitution shall be made from that time until play has been resumed. The home team may then make any desired substitution which do not result in the delay of the game.

If there is any undue delay by either team in changing lines, the Referee shall order the offending team or teams to take their positions immediately and not permit a line change.

(NOTE) *When a substitution has been made under the above rule no additional substitution may be made until play commences.*

Rule 17.   **Equalizing of Teams**
                                        D E L E T E D

Rule 18.   **Change of Players**
(a) Players may be changed at any time from the players' bench, provided that the player or players leaving the ice shall always be at the players' bench and out of the play before any change is made.

A goalkeeper may be changed for another player at any time under the conditions set out in this section.

(NOTE 1) *When a goalkeeper leaves his goal area and proceeds to his players' bench for the purpose of substituting another player, the rear Linesman shall be responsible to see that the substitution made is not illegal by reason of the premature departure of the substitute from the bench (before the goalkeeper is within ten feet of the bench). If the substitution is made prematurely, the Linesman shall stop the play immediately by blowing his whistle unless the non-offending team has possession of the puck in which event the stoppage will be delayed until the puck changes hands. There shall be no time penalty to the team making the premature substitution but the resulting face-off will take place on the center "face-off spot."*

(NOTE 2) *If in the course of making a substitution the player entering the game plays the puck with his stick, skates or hands or who checks or makes any physical contact with an opposing player while the retiring player is actually on the ice then infraction of "too many men on the ice" will be called.*

If in the course of a substitution either the player entering the play or the player retiring is struck by the puck accidentally, the play will not be stopped and no penalty will be called.

(b) If by reason of insufficient playing time remaining, or by reason of penalties already imposed, a bench minor penalty is imposed for deliberate illegal substitution (too many men on the ice) which cannot be served in its entirety within the legal playing time, a penalty shot shall be awarded against the offending team.

(c) A player serving a penalty on the penalty bench, who is to be changed after the penalty has been served, must proceed at once by way of the ice and be at his own players' bench before any change can be made.

For any violation of this rule a bench minor penalty shall be imposed.

Rule 19.   **Injured Players**

(a) When a player, other than a goalkeeper, is injured or compelled to leave the ice during a game, he may retire from the game and be replaced by a substitute, but play must continue without the teams leaving the ice.

(b) If a goalkeeper sustains an injury or becomes ill, he must be ready to resume play immediately or be replaced by a substitute goalkeeper and NO additional time shall be allowed by the referee for the purpose of enabling the injured or ill goalkeeper to resume his position. (See also Section (d).)

(c) The Referee shall report to the President for disciplinary action any delay in making a goalkeeper substitution.

The substitute goalkeeper shall be subject to the regular rules governing goalkeepers and shall be entitled to the same privileges.

(d) When a substitution for the regular goalkeeper has been made, such regular goalkeeper shall not resume his position until the first stoppage of play thereafter.

(e) If a penalized player has been injured, he may proceed to the dressing room without the necessity of taking a seat on the penalty bench. If the injured player receives a minor penalty, the penalized team shall immediately put a substitute player on the penalty bench who shall serve the penalty without change. If the injured player receives a major penalty, the penalized team shall place a substitute player on the penalty bench before the penalty expires and no other replacement for the penalized player shall be permitted to enter the game except from the penalty bench. For violation of this rule a bench minor penalty shall be imposed.

The penalized player who has been injured and been replaced on the penalty bench shall not be eligible to play until his penalty has expired.

(f) When a player is injured so that he cannot continue play or go to his bench, the play shall not be stopped until the injured players' team has secured possession of the puck; if the player's team is in possession of the puck at the time of injury, play shall be stopped immediately, unless his team is in a scoring position.

(NOTE) *In the case where it is obvious that a player has sustained a serious injury the Referee and/or Linesman may stop the play immediately.*

SECTION THREE—EQUIPMENT

Rule 20.   **Sticks**

(a) The sticks shall be made of wood or other material approved by the Rules Committee, and must not have any projections. Adhesive tape of any colour may be wrapped around the stick at any place for the purpose of reinforcement or to improve control of the puck.

(b) No stick shall exceed fifty-five inches in length from the heel to the end of the shaft nor more than twelve and one-half inches from the heel to the end of the blade.

The blade of the stick shall not be more than three inches in width at any point nor less than two inches. All edges of the blade of the stick shall be bevelled. The curvature of the blade of the stick shall be restricted in such a way that the distance of a perpendicular line measured from a straight line drawn from any point at the heel to the end of the blade to the point of maximum curvature shall not exceed one-half inch.

(c) The blade of the goalkeeper's stick shall not exceed three and one-half inches in width at any point except at the heel where it must not exceed four and one-half inches in width; nor shall the goalkeeper's stick exceed fifteen and one-half inches in length from the heel to the end of the blade.

The widened portion of the goalkeeper's stick extending up the shaft from the blade shall not extend more than twenty-six inches from the heel and shall not exceed three and one-half inches in width.

(d) A minor penalty plus a fine of two hundred dollars ($200.00) shall be imposed on any player or goalkeeper who uses a stick not conforming to the provisions of this rule.

(NOTE 1) *When a formal complaint is made by the Captain or Alternate Captain of a team, against the dimensions of any stick, the Referee shall take the stick to the Timekeeper's bench where the necessary measurement shall be made immediately. The result shall be reported to the Penalty Timekeeper who shall record it on the back of the penalty record.*

If the complaint is not sustained a fine of one hundred dollars ($100.00) shall be imposed against the complaining club by the President.

(NOTE 2) *A player, who participates in the play while taking a replacement stick to his goalkeeper shall incur a minor penalty under this rule but the automatic fine of two hundred dollars ($200.00) shall not be imposed. If his participation causes a foul resulting in a minor or major penalty, the referee shall report the incident to the President for disciplinary action.*

(e) In the event that a player scores on a penalty shot while using an illegal stick the goal shall be disallowed and no further penalty imposed. However, if no goal is scored, the player taking the penalty shot shall receive a minor penalty.

(f) A minor penalty plus a ten-minute misconduct penalty shall be imposed on any player who refuses to surrender his stick for measurement when requested to do so by the Referee. In addition this player shall be subject to a $200 fine.

Rule 21.   **Skates**

(a) All hockey skates shall be of a design approved by the Rules Committee. All skates worn by players (but not goalkeepers) and by the Referee and Linesmen shall be equipped with approved safety heel tips.

When the Referee becomes aware that any person is wearing a skate on which the protective heel tip is missing or broken, he shall direct its replacement at the next intermission. If such replacement is not carried out, the Referee shall report the incident to the President for disciplinary action.

(b) The use of speed skates or fancy skates or any skate so designed that it may cause injury is prohibited.

Rule 22.   **Goalkeeper's Equipment**

(a) With the exception of skates and stick, all the equipment worn by the goalkeeper must be constructed solely for the purpose of protecting the head or body, and he must not wear any garment or use any contrivance which would give him undue assistance in keeping goal.

(NOTE) *Cages on gloves and abdominal aprons extending down the front of the thighs on the outside of the pants are prohibited. "Cage" shall mean any lacing or webbing or other material in the goalkeeper's glove joining the thumb and index finger which is in excess of the minimum necessary to fill the gap when the goalkeeper's thumb and forefinger in the glove are fully extended and spread and includes any pocket or pouch effect produced by excess lacing or webbing or other material between the thumb and forefinger when fully extended or spread.*

Protective padding attached to the back or forming part of goalkeeper's gloves shall not exceed eight inches in width nor more than sixteen inches in length at any point.

(b) The leg guards worn by goalkeepers shall not exceed ten inches in extreme width when on the leg of the player.

(NOTE) *At the commencement of each season and prior to play-offs goalkeepers' leg guards shall be checked by League Staff and any violation of this rule shall be reported to the club involved and to the President of the League.*

(c) Protective masks of a design approved by the Rules Committee may be worn by goalkeepers.

Rule 23.   Protective Equipment

All protective equipment, except gloves, headgear and goalkeeper's leg guards, must be worn under the uniform.

For violation of this rule after warning by the Referee a minor penalty shall be imposed.

(NOTE) *Players including the goalkeeper violating this rule shall not be permitted to participate in game until such equipment has been corrected or removed.*

Rule 24.   Dangerous Equipment

(a) The use of pads or protectors made of metal, or of any other material likely to cause injury to a player, is prohibited.

(b) A mask or protector of a design approved by the Rules Committee may be worn by a player who has sustained a facial injury.

(NOTE) *All elbow pads which do not have a soft protective outer covering of sponge rubber or similar material at least ½ inch thick shall be considered dangerous equipment.*

In the first instance the injured player shall be entitled to wear any protective device prescribed by the club doctor. If any opposing club objects to the device it may record its objection with the President who shall promptly poll the Rules Committee for approval or otherwise.

(c) A glove from which all or part of the palm has been removed or cut to permit the use of the bare hand shall be considered illegal equipment and if any player wears such a glove in play a minor penalty shall be imposed on him.

(NOTE) *The Referee-in-Chief is specifically authorized to make a check of each team's equipment to ensure the compliance with this rule. He shall report his findings to the President for his disciplinary action.*

Rule 25.   Puck

(a) The puck shall be made of vulcanized rubber, or other approved material, one inch thick and three inches in diameter and shall weigh between five and a half ounces and six ounces. All pucks used in competition must be approved by the Rules Committee.

(b) The home team shall be responsible for providing an adequate supply of official pucks which shall be kept in a frozen condition. This supply of pucks shall be kept at the penalty bench under the control of one of the regular minor officials or a special attendant.

(NOTE) *As of June 10, 1969, pucks manufactured by the Converse Rubber Co. and the Viceroy Manufacturing Co. have been approved by the Rules Committee.*

(NOTE TO SECTION THREE) *A request for measurement of any equipment covered by this section shall be limited to one request by each club during the course of any stoppage of play.*

The Referee may, at his own discretion, measure any equipment used for the first time in the game.

SECTION FOUR—PENALTIES

Rule 26.   **Penalties**

Penalties shall be actual playing time and shall be divided into the following classes:

               (1) Minor Penalties
               (2) Bench Minor Penalties
               (3) Major Penalties
               (4) Misconduct Penalties
               (5) Match Penalties
               (6) Penalty Shot

Where coincident penalties are imposed on players of both teams the penalized players of the visiting team shall take their positions on the penalty bench first in the place designated for visiting players.

(NOTE) *When play is not actually in progress and an offense is committed by any player, the same penalty shall apply as though play were actually in progress.*

Rule 27.   **Minor Penalties**

(a) For a "MINOR PENALTY," any player, other than a goalkeeper, shall be ruled off the ice for two minutes during which time no substitute shall be permitted.

(b) A "BENCH MINOR" penalty involves the removal from

the ice of one player of the team against which the penalty is awarded for a period of two minutes. Any player except a goalkeeper of the team may be designated to serve the penalty by the Manager or Coach through the playing Captain and such player shall take his place on the penalty bench promptly and serve the penalty as if it was a minor penalty imposed upon him.

(c) If while a team is "short-handed" by one or more minor or bench minor penalties the opposing team scores a goal, the first of such penalties shall automatically terminate.

(NOTE 1) *"Short-handed" means that the team must be below the numerical strength of its opponents on the ice at the time the goal is scored. The minor or bench minor penalty which terminates automatically is the one which causes the team scored against to be "short-handed" originally (first penalty). Thus coincident minor penalties to both teams do NOT cause either side to be "short-handed."*

This rule shall also apply when a goal is scored on a penalty shot.

When the minor penalties of two players of the same team terminate at the same time the Captain of that team shall designate to the Referee which of such players will return to the ice first and the Referee will instruct the Penalty Timekeeper accordingly.

When a player receives a major penalty and a minor penalty at the same time the major penalty shall be served first by the penalized player except under Rule 28(c) in which case the minor penalty will be recorded and served first.

(NOTE 2): *This applies to the case where BOTH penalties are imposed on the SAME player.*

See also Note to Rule 33.

Rule 28.   Major Penalties

(a) For the first "MAJOR PENALTY" in any one game, the offender, except the goalkeeper, shall be ruled off the ice for five minutes, during which time no substitute shall be permitted.

An automatic fine of fifty dollars ($50.00) shall also be added when a major penalty is imposed for any foul causing injury to the face or head of an opponent by means of a stick.

(b) For the third major penalty in the same game, to the same player, he shall be ruled off the ice for the balance of the playing time, but a substitute shall be permitted to replace the player so suspended after five minutes shall have elapsed. (Major penalty plus game misconduct penalty with automatic fine of one hundred dollars ($100.00).)

(c) When coincident major penalties or coincident penalties of equal duration, including a major penalty, are imposed against players of both teams, the penalized players shall all take their places on the penalty benches and such penalized players shall not leave the penalty bench until the first stoppage of play following the expiry of their respective penalties. Immediate substitutions shall be made for an equal number of major penalties or *coincident penalties of equal duration including a major penalty* to each team so penalized and the penalties of the players *for* which substitution have been made shall not be taken into account for the purpose of the delayed Rule 33.

Where it is required to determine which of the penalized players shall be designated to serve the delayed penalty under Rule 33 the penalized team shall have the right to make such designation not in conflict with Rule 27.

Rule 29.   **Misconduct Penalties**

(a) "MISCONDUCT" penalties to all players except the goalkeeper, involve removal from the game for a period of ten minutes each. A substitute player is permitted to immediately replace a player serving a misconduct penalty. A player whose misconduct penalty has expired shall remain in the penalty box until the next stoppage of play.

When a player receives a minor penalty and a misconduct penalty at the same time, the penalized team shall immediately put a substitute player on the penalty bench and he shall serve the minor penalty without change.

When a player receives a major penalty and a misconduct penalty at the same time, the penalized team shall place a substitute player on the penalty bench before the major penalty expires and no replacement for the penalized player shall be permitted to enter the game except from the penalty bench. Any violation of this provision shall be treated as an illegal substitution under Rule 18 calling for a bench minor penalty.

(b) A misconduct penalty imposed on any player at any time, shall be accompanied with an automatic fine of fifty dollars ($50.00).

(c) A "GAME MISCONDUCT" penalty involves the suspension of a player for the balance of the game but a substitute is permitted to replace immediately the player so removed. A player incurring a game misconduct penalty shall incur an automatic fine of one hundred dollars ($100.00) and the case shall be reported to the President who shall have full power to impose such further penalties by way of suspension or fine on the penalized player or any other player involved in the altercation.

(NOTE) *For all "Game Misconduct" penalties, regardless of when imposed, a total of ten minutes shall be charged in the records against the offending player.*

(d) A game misconduct penalty shall be imposed on any player or goalkeeper on the ice who is the first to intervene in an altercation then in progress. This penalty is in addition to any other penalty incurred in the same incident.

(e) The Referee may impose a gross misconduct penalty on any player, Manager, Coach, or Trainer who is guilty of gross misconduct of any kind, including but not limited to hair-pulling, spitting, biting. Any person incurring a game misconduct penalty shall be suspended for the balance of the game and shall incur an automatic fine of one hundred dollars ($100), and the case shall be referred to the President of the League for further action.

(NOTE) *For all game misconduct and gross misconduct penalties regardless of when imposed, a total of ten minutes shall be charged in the records against the offensive player.*

(f) In regular League games, any player who incurs a total of three game misconduct and/or gross misconduct penalties shall be suspended automatically for the next League game of his team. For each subsequent game misconduct or gross misconduct penalty the automatic suspension shall be increased by one game. For each suspension of a player, his club shall be fined one thousand dollars ($1,000).

In play-off games, any player who incurs a total of two game misconduct and/or gross misconduct penalties shall be suspended automatically for the next play-off game of his team. For each subsequent game misconduct or gross misconduct penalty during the play-offs, the automatic suspension shall be increased by one game. For each suspension of a player during the play-offs, his club shall be fined one thousand dollars ($1,000).

(NOTE) *Any game misconduct or gross misconduct penalty for which a player has been assessed supplementary discipline in the form of game suspension(s) by the President shall not be taken into account when calculating the total number of offences under this sub-section.*

Rule 30.   **Match Penalties**

(a) A "MATCH" penalty involves the suspension of a player for the balance of the game, and the offender shall be ordered to the dressing room immediately. A substitute player is permitted to replace the penalized player after ten minutes playing time has elapsed when the penalty is imposed under Rule 49, and after five minutes actual playing time has elapsed when the penalty is imposed under Rule 44.

(NOTE 1) *Regulations regarding additional penalties and substitutes are specifically covered in individual Rules 44, 49 and 64; any additional penalty shall be served by a player to be designated by the Manager or Coach of the offending team through the playing Captain such player to take his place in the penalty box immediately.*

For all "MATCH" penalties, regardless of when imposed, or prescribed additional penalties, a total of ten minutes shall be charged in the records against the offending player.

(NOTE 2) *When the coincident match penalties have been imposed under Rule 44, Rule 49 or Rule 64 to a player on both teams Rule 28 (c) covering coincident major penalties will be applicable with respect to player substitution.*

(b) A player incurring a match penalty shall incur an automatic fine of two hundred dollars ($200.00) and the case shall be investigated promptly by the President who shall have full power to impose such further penalty by way of suspension or fine on the penalized player or any other player involved in the altercation.

(NOTE) *The Referee is required to report all match penalties and the surrounding circumstances to the President of the League immediately following the game in which they occur.*

Rule 31.   **Penalty Shot**

(a) Any infraction of the rules which calls for a "Penalty Shot" shall be taken as follows:—

The Referee shall cause to be announced over the public address system the name of the player designated by him or selected by the team entitled to take the shot (as appropriate) and shall then place the puck on the center face-off spot and the player taking the shot will, on the instruction of the Referee, play the puck from there and shall attempt to score on the goalkeeper. The player taking the shot may carry the puck in any part of the Neutral Zone or his own Defending Zone but once the puck has crossed the Attacking Blue Line it must be kept in motion towards the opponent's goal line and once it is shot the play shall be considered complete. No goal can be scored on a rebound of any kind and any time the puck crosses the goal line the shot shall be considered complete.

Only a player designated as a goalkeeper or alternate goalkeeper may defend against the penalty shot.

(b) The goalkeeper must remain in his crease until the player taking the penalty shot has touched the puck and in the event of violation of this rule or any foul committed by a goalkeeper the Referee shall allow the shot to be taken and if the shot fails he shall permit the penalty shot to be taken over again.

The goalkeeper may attempt to stop the shot in any manner except by throwing his stick or any object, in which case a goal shall be awarded.

(NOTE) *See Rule 80.*

(c) In cases where a penalty shot has been awarded under Rule 62(g)—Interference, under Rule 66(k)—for illegal entry into the game, under Rule 80(a) —for throwing a stick and under Rule 83(b)—for fouling from behind, the Referee shall designate the player who has been fouled as the player who shall take the penalty shot.

In cases where a penalty shot has been awarded under Rule 18(b)—deliberate illegal substitution with insufficient playing time remaining or Rule 50(c)—deliberately displacing goal post or Rule 53(c)—falling on the puck in the crease or Rule 57(d)—picking up the puck from the crease area— the penalty shot shall be taken by a player selected by the Captain of the non-offending team from the players on the ice at the time when the foul was committed. Such selection shall be reported to the Referee and cannot be changed.

If by reason of injury the player designated by the Referee to take the penalty shot is unable to do so within a reasonable time, the shot may be taken by a player selected by the Captain of the non-offending team from the players on the ice when the foul was committed. Such selection shall be reported to the Referee and cannot be changed.

(d) Should the player in respect to whom a penalty shot has been awarded himself commit a foul in connection with the same play or circumstances, either before or after the penalty shot penalty has been awarded, be designated to take the shot he shall first be permitted to do so before being sent to the penalty bench to serve the penalty except when such a penalty is for a game misconduct or match penalty in which case the penalty shot shall be taken by a player selected by the Captain of the non-offending team from the players on the ice at the time when the foul was committed.

If at the time a penalty shot is awarded the goalkeeper of the penalized team has been removed from the ice to substitute another player, the goalkeeper shall be permitted to return to the ice before the penalty shot is taken.

(e) While the penalty shot is being taken, players of both sides shall withdraw to the sides of the rink and beyond the center red line.

(f) If, while the penalty shot is being taken, any player of the opposing team shall have by some action interfered with or distracted the player taking the shot and because of such action the shot should have failed, a second attempt shall be permitted and the Referee shall impose a misconduct penalty on the player so interfering or distracting.

(g) If a goal is scored from a penalty shot the puck shall be faced at center ice in the usual way. If a goal is not scored the puck shall be faced at either of the end face-off spots in the zone in which the penalty shot has been tried.

(h) Should a goal be scored from a penalty shot, a further penalty to the offending player shall not be applied unless the offense for which the penalty shot was awarded was such as to incur a major or match penalty or misconduct penalty, in which case the penalty prescribed for the particular offense, shall be imposed.

If the offense for which the penalty shot was awarded was such as would normally incur a minor penalty, then regardless of whether the penalty shot results in a goal or not, no further minor penalty shall be served.

(i) If the foul upon which the penalty shot is based occurs during actual playing time, the penalty shot shall be awarded and taken immediately in the usual manner notwithstanding any delay occasioned by a slow whistle by the Referee to permit the play to be completed which delay results in the expiry of the regular playing time in any period.

The time required for the taking of a penalty shot shall not be included in the regular playing time or any overtime.

Rule 32. **Goalkeeper's Penalties**

(a) A goalkeeper shall not be sent to the penalty bench for an offense which incurs a minor penalty, but instead the minor penalty shall be served by another member of his team who was on the ice when the offense was committed, said player to be designated by the Manager or Coach of the offending team through the playing Captain and such substitute shall not be changed.

(b) Same as 32(a) above except change "minor" to "major."

(c) Should a goalkeeper incur three major penalties in one game he shall be ruled off the ice for the balance of the playing time and his place will be taken by a member of his own club, or by a regular substitute goalkeeper who is available. (Major penalty plus game misconduct penalty and automatic fine of one hundred dollars ($100.00).)

(d) Should a goalkeeper on the ice incur a misconduct penalty this penalty shall be served by another member of his team who was on the ice when the offense was committed, said player to be designated by the Manager or Coach of the offending team through the playing Captain and, in addition, the goalkeeper shall be fined fifty dollars ($50.00).

(e) Should a goalkeeper incur a game misconduct penalty, his place then will be taken by a member of his own club, or by a regular substitute goalkeeper who is available, and such player will be allowed the goalkeeper's full equipment. In addition the goalkeeper shall be fined one hundred dollars ($100.00).

(f) Should a goalkeeper incur a match penalty, his place then will be taken by a member of his own club, or by a substitute goalkeeper who is available, and such player will be allowed the goalkeeper's equipment. However, any additional penalties as specifically called for by the individual rules covering match penalties, will apply, and the offending team shall be penalized accordingly; such additional penalty to be served by another member of the team on the ice at the time the offense was committed, said player to be designated by the Manager or Coach of the offending team through the playing Captain. (See Rules 44, 49 and 64.)

(g) A goalkeeper incurring a match penalty shall incur an automatic fine of two hundred dollars ($200.00) and the case

shall be investigated promptly by the President who shall
have full power to impose such further penalty by way of
suspension or fine on the penalized goalkeeper or any other
player in the altercation.

(h) A minor penalty shall be imposed on a goalkeeper who
leaves the immediate vicinity of his crease during an altercation. In addition, he shall be subject to a fine of one hundred dollars ($100.00) and this incident shall be reported to
the President for such further disciplinary action as may be
required.

(NOTE) *All penalties imposed on a goalkeeper regardless
of who serves penalty or any substitution, shall be charged
in the records against the goalkeeper.*

(i) If a goalkeeper participates in the play in any manner when
he is beyond the center red line a minor penalty shall be imposed upon him.

Rule 33.   **Delayed Penalties**

(a) If a third player of any team shall be penalized while two
players of the same team are serving penalties, the penalty
time of the third player shall not commence until the penalty time of one of the two players already penalized shall
have elapsed. Nevertheless, the third player penalized must
at once proceed to the penalty bench but may be replaced
by a substitute until such time as the penalty time of the
penalized player shall commence.

(b) When any team shall have three players serving penalties at
the same time and because of the delayed penalty rule, a
substitute for the third offender is on the ice, none of the
three penalized players on the penalty bench may return to
the ice until play has been stopped. When play has been
stopped, the player whose full penalty has expired, may return to the play.

Provided however that the Penalty Timekeeper shall permit
the return to the ice in the order of expiry of their penalties,
of a player or players when by reason of the expiration of
their penalties the penalized team is entitled to have more
than four players on the ice.

(c) In the case of delayed penalties, the Referee shall instruct
the Penalty Timekeeper that penalized players whose penalties have expired shall only be allowed to return to the ice
when there is a stoppage of play.

When the penalties of two players of the same team will

expire at the same time the Captain of that team will designate to the Referee which of such players will return to the ice first and the Referee will instruct the Penalty Timekeeper accordingly.

When a major and a minor penalty are imposed at the same time on players of the same team the Penalty Timekeeper shall record the minor as being the first of such penalties.

(NOTE) *This applies to the case where the two penalties are imposed on DIFFERENT players of the same team. See also Note to Rule 27.*

Rule 34.   **Calling of Penalties**

(a) Should an infraction of the rules which would call for a minor, major, misconduct, game misconduct or match penalty be committed by a player of the side in possession of the puck, the Referee shall immediately blow his whistle and give the penalties to the deserving players.

The resulting face-off shall be made at the place where the play was stopped unless the stoppage occurs in the Attacking Zone of the player penalized in which case the face-off shall be made at the nearest face-off spot in the Neutral Zone.

In addition to the automatic fines and suspensions imposed under these rules, the President may, at his discretion, investigate any incident that occurs in connection with any league or play-off game and may assess additional fines and/or suspensions for any offense committed during the course of a game or any aftermath thereof by a player, Trainer, Manager, Coach or Club Executive whether or not such offense has been penalized by the Referee.

(b) Should an infraction of the rules which would call for a minor, major, misconduct, game misconduct or match penalty be committed by a player of the team not in possession of the puck, the Referee will blow his whistle and impose the penalty on the offending player upon completion of the play by the team in possession of the puck.

(NOTE) *There shall be no signal given by the Referee for a misconduct or game misconduct penalty under this section.*

The resulting face-off shall be made at the place where the play was stopped, unless during the period of a delayed whistle due to a foul by a player of the side NOT in possession, the side in possession ices the puck, shoots the puck so that it goes out of bounds or is unplayable then the face-off following the stoppage shall take place in the Neutral Zone near the Defending Blue Line of the team shooting the puck.

If the penalty or penalties to be imposed are minor penalties and a goal is scored on the play by the non-offending side, the minor penalty or penalties shall not be imposed but major and match penalties shall be imposed in the normal manner regardless of whether a goal is scored or not.

(NOTE 1) *"Completion of the play by the team in possession" in this rule means that the puck must have come into the possession and control of an opposing player or has been "frozen." This does not mean a rebound off the goalkeeper, the goal or the boards or any accidental contact with the body or equipment of an opposing player.*

(NOTE 2) *If after the Referee has signalled a penalty but before the whistle has been blown the puck shall enter the goal of the non-offending team as the direct result of the action of a player of that team, the goal shall be allowed and the penalty signalled shall be imposed in the normal manner.*

If when a team is "short-handed" by reason of one or more minor or bench minor penalties the Referee signals a further minor penalty or penalties against the "short-handed" team and a goal is scored by the non-offending side before the whistle is blown then the goal shall be allowed, the penalty or penalties signalled shall be washed out and the first of the minor penalties already being served shall automatically terminate under Rule 27(c).

(c) Should the same offending player commit other fouls on the same play, either before or after the Referee has blown his whistle, the offending player shall serve such penalties consecutively.

SECTION FIVE—OFFICIALS

Rule 35. **Appointment of Officials**

(a) The President shall appoint a Referee, two Linesmen, Game Timekeeper, Penalty Timekeeper, Official Scorer and two Goal Judges for each game.

(b) The President shall forward to all clubs a list of Referees, and Minor Officials, all of whom must be treated with

proper respect at all times during the season by all players
and officials of clubs.

Rule 36.   **Referee**

(a) The REFEREE shall have general supervision of the game,
and shall have full control of all game officials and players
during the game, including stoppages; and in case of any
dispute, his decision shall be final. The Referee shall remain
on the ice at the conclusion of each period until all players
have proceeded to their dressing rooms.

(b) All Referees and Linesmen shall be garbed in black trousers
and official sweaters.

   They shall be equipped with approved whistles and metal
tape measures with minimum length of six feet.

(c) The Referee shall order the teams on the ice at the appointed time for the beginning of a game and at the commencement of each period. If for any reason there be more
than fifteen minutes' delay in the commencement of the
game or any undue delay in resuming play after the fifteen
minute intervals between periods, the Referee shall state in
his report to the President the cause of the delay, and the
club or clubs which were at fault.

(d) It shall be his duty to see to it that all players are properly
dressed, and that the approved regulation equipment is in
use at all times during the game.

(e) The Referee shall, before starting the game, see that the appointed Game Timekeeper, Penalty Timekeeper, Official
Scorer and Goal Judges are in their respective places, and
satisfy himself that the timing and signalling equipment are
in order.

(f) It shall be his duty to impose such penalties as are
prescribed by the rules for infractions thereof, and he shall
give the final decision in matters of disputed goals. The Referee may consult with the Linesmen or Goal Judge before
making his decision.

(g) The Referee shall announce to the Official Scorer or Penalty
Timekeeper all goals legally scored as well as penalties, and
for what infractions such penalties are imposed.

   The Referee shall cause to be announced over the public
address system the reason for not allowing a goal every time
the goal signal light is turned on in the course of play. This
shall be done at the first stoppage of play regardless of any

standard signal given by the Referee when the goal signal light was put on in error.

The Referee shall report to the Official Scorer the name or number of the goal scorer but he shall *not* give any information or advice with respect to assists.

(NOTE) *The name of the scorer and any player entitled to an assist will be announced on the public address system. In the event that the Referee disallows a goal for any violation of the rules, he shall report the reason for disallowance to the Official Scorer who shall announce the Referee's decision correctly over the public address system.*

The infraction of the rules for which each penalty has been imposed will be announced correctly, as reported by the Referee, over the public address system. Where players of both teams are penalized on the same play, the penalty to the visiting player will be announced first.

Where a penalty is imposed by the Referee which calls for a mandatory or automatic fine, only the time portion of the penalty will be reported by the Referee to the Official Scorer and announced on the public address system, and the fine will be collected through the League office.

(h) The Referee shall see to it that players of opposing teams are separated on the penalty bench to prevent feuding.

(i) He shall not halt the game for any infractions of the rules concerning off-side play at the blue line, or center lines or any violation of the "icing the puck" rule which shall be the function of the Linesman alone, unless the Linesman shall be prevented by some accident from doing so, in which case the duties of the Linesman shall be assumed by the Referee until play is stopped.

(j) Should a Referee accidentally leave the ice or receive an injury which incapacitates him from discharging his duties while play is in progress the game shall be automatically stopped.

(k) If, through misadventure or sickness, the Referee and Linesmen appointed are prevented from appearing, the Managers or Coaches of the two clubs shall agree on a Referee and Linesman. If they are unable to agree, they shall appoint a player from each side who shall act as Referee and Linesman; the player of the home club acting as Referee, and the player of the visiting club as Linesman.

(l) If the regularly appointed officials appear during the progress of the game, they shall at once replace the temporary officials.

(m) Should a Linesman appointed be unable to act at the last minute or through sickness or accident be unable to finish the game, the Referee shall have the power to appoint another, in his stead, if he deems it necessary, or if required to do so by the Manager or Coach of either of the competing teams.

(n) If, owing to illness or accident, the Referee is unable to continue to officiate, one of the Linesmen shall perform such duties as devolved upon the Referee during the balance of the game, the Linesman to be selected by the Referee.

(o) The Referee shall check club's rosters and all players in uniform before signing reports of the game.

(p) The Referee shall report to the President promptly and in detail the circumstances of any of the following incidents:—

   (1) When a stick or part thereof is thrown outside the playing area;

   (2) Every obscene gesture made by any person involved in the playing or conduct of the game whether as a participant or as an official of either team or of the League, which gesture he has personally observed or which has been brought to his attention by any game official;

   (3) When any player, Trainer, Coach or Club Executive becomes involved in an altercation with a spectator.

   (4) Every infraction under Rule 77(c) (slashing).

Rule 37.   **Linesman**

(a) The duty of the LINESMAN is to determine any infractions of the rules concerning off-side play at the blue line, or center line, or any violation of the "icing the puck" rule.

   He shall stop the play when the puck goes outside the playing area and when it is interfered with by any ineligible person and when it is struck above the height of the shoulder and when the goal post has been displaced from its normal position. He shall stop the play for off-sides occurring on face-offs circles. He shall stop the play when there has been a premature substitution for a goalkeeper under Rule 18(a) and for Injured Players under Rule 19(f) and Interference by Spectators under Rule 63(a).

(b) He shall face the puck at all times, except at the start of the game, at the beginning of each period and after a goal has been scored.

   The Referee may call upon a Linesman to conduct a face-off at any time.

(c) He shall, when requested to do so by the Referee, give his version of any incident that may have taken place during the playing of the game.

(d) He shall not stop the play to impose any penalty except any violation of the Rule 18(a) & (c)—Change of Players (too many men on the ice) and any violation of Rule 42(h) (articles thrown on the ice from vicinity of players' or penalty bench) and Rule 46(c) (stick thrown on ice from players' bench) and he shall report such violation to the Referee who shall impose a bench minor penalty against the offending team.

He shall report immediately to the Referee his version of the circumstances with respect to Rule 50(c)—Delaying the game by deliberately displacing post from its normal position.

He shall report immediately to the Referee his version of any infraction of the rules constituting a major or match foul or game misconduct or any conduct calling for a bench minor penalty or misconduct penalty under these rules.

Rule 38.   **Goal Judge**
(a) There shall be one GOAL JUDGE at each goal. They shall not be members of either club engaged in a game, nor shall they be replaced during its progress, unless after the commencement of the game it becomes apparent that either Goal Judge, on account of partisanship or any other cause, is guilty of giving unjust decisions, when the Referee may appoint another Goal Judge to act in his stead.

(b) Goal Judges shall be stationed behind the goals, during the progress of play, in properly screened cages, so that there can be no interference with their activities; and they shall not change goals during the game.

(c) In the event of a goal being claimed, the Goal Judge of that goal shall decide whether or not the puck has passed between the goal posts and entirely over the goal line, his decision simply being "goal" or "no goal."

Rule 39.   **Penalty Timekeeper**
(a) The PENALTY TIMEKEEPER shall keep, on the official forms provided, a correct record of all penalties imposed by the officials including the names of the players penalized, the infractions penalized, the duration of each penalty and the time at which each penalty was imposed. He shall report

in the Penalty Record each penalty shot awarded, the name of the player taking the shot and the result of the shot.

(b) The Penalty Timekeeper shall check and ensure that the time served by all penalized players is correct. He shall be responsible for the correct posting of penalties on the scoreboard at all times and shall promptly call to the attention of the Referee any discrepancy between the time recorded on the clock and the official correct time and he shall be responsible for making any adjustments ordered by the Referee.

He shall upon request, give a penalized player correct information as to the unexpired time of his penalty.

(NOTE 1) *The infraction of the rules for which each penalty has been imposed will be announced twice over the public address system as reported by the Referee. Where players of both teams are penalized on the same play, the penalty to the visiting player will be announced first.*

(NOTE 2) *Misconduct penalties and co-incident major penalties should not be recorded on the timing device but such penalized players should be alerted and released at the first stoppage of play following the expiration of their penalties.*

(c) Upon the completion of each game, the Penalty Timekeeper shall complete and sign three copies of the Penalty Record to be distributed as quickly as possible to the following persons:—

(1) One copy to the Official Scorer for transmission to the League President;

(2) One copy to the visiting Coach or Manager;

(3) One copy to the home Coach or Manager.

(d) The Referee-in-Chief shall be entitled to inspect, collect and forward to the League headquarters the actual work sheets used by the Penalty Timekeeper in any game.

Rule 40.   **Official Scorer**

(a) Before the start of the game, the Official Scorer shall obtain from the Manager or Coach of both teams a list of all eligible players and the starting line-up of each team which information shall be made known to the opposing team Manager or Coach before the start of play either personally or through the Referee.

The Official Scorer shall secure the names of the Captain, from the Manager or Coach at the time the line-ups are

collected and will indicate those nominated by placing the
letter "C" opposite their names on the Referee's Report of
Match. All of this information shall be presented to the Referee for his signature at the completion of the game.

(b) The Official Scorer shall keep a record of the goals scored,
the scorers, and players to whom assists have been credited,
and shall indicate those players on the lists who have actually taken part in the game. He shall also record the time of
entry into the game of any substitute goalkeeper. He shall
record on the Official Score Sheet a notation where a goal is
scored when the goalkeeper has been removed from the ice.

(c) The Official Scorer shall award the points for goals and assists and his decision shall be final. The awards of points for
goals and assists shall be announced twice over the public
address system and all changes in such awards shall also be
announced in the same manner.

No requests for changes in any award of points shall be
considered unless they are made at or before the conclusion
of actual play in the game by the team Captain.

(d) At the conclusion of the game the Official Scorer shall complete and sign three copies of the Official Score Sheet for
distribution as quickly as possible to the following persons:—

   (1) One copy to the League President;
   (2) One copy to the visiting Coach or Manager;
   (3) One copy to the home Coach or Manager.

(e) The Official Scorer shall also prepare the Official Report of
Match for signature by the Referee and forward it to the
League President together with the Official Score Sheet and
the Penalty Record.

(f) The Official Scorer should be in an elevated position, well
away from the players' benches, with house telephone communication to the Public Address Announcer.

Rule 41.   **Game Timekeeper**

(a) The Game Timekeeper shall record the time of starting and
finishing of each period in the game and all playing time
during the game.

(b) The Game Timekeeper shall signal the Referee and the
competing teams for the start of the game and each succeeding period and the Referee shall start the play promptly in
accordance with Rule 81.

To assist in assuring the prompt return to the ice of the

teams and the officials the Game Timekeeper shall give a preliminary warning three minutes prior to the resumption of play in each period.

(c) If the rink is not equipped with an automatic gong or bell or siren or, if such device fails to function, the Game Timekeeper shall signal the end of each period by ringing a gong or bell or by blowing a whistle.

(d) He shall cause to be announced on the public address system at the nineteenth minute in each period that there is one minute remaining to be played in the period.

(e) In the event of any dispute regarding time, the matter shall be referred to the Referee for adjustment, and his decision shall be final.

Rule 41A.   Statistician

(a) There shall be appointed for duty at every game played in the League a Statistician and such assistants or alternates as may be deemed necessary.

(b) The duty of the Statistician(s) is to correctly record on the official League forms supplied all of the data therein provided for concerning the performances of the individual players and the participating teams.

(c) These records shall be compiled and recorded in strict conformity with the instructions printed on the forms supplied and shall be completed as to totals where required and with such accuracy as to ensure that the data supplied is "in balance."

(d) At the conclusion of each game the Statistician shall sign and distribute three copies of the final and correct Statistician's Report to each of the following persons:—

   (1) One copy to the League President (through the Official Scorer if possible—otherwise by direct mail);
   (2) One copy to the visiting Coach or Manager;
   (3) One copy to the home Coach or Manager.

SECTION SIX—PLAYING RULES

Rule 42.   Abuse of Officials and other Misconduct

(NOTE) *In the enforcement of this rule the Referee has, in many instances, the option of imposing a "misconduct pen-*

alty" or a "bench minor penalty." In principle the Referee is directed to impose a "bench minor penalty" in respect to the violations which occur on or in the immediate vicinity of the players' bench but off the playing surface, and in all cases affecting non-playing personnel or players. A "misconduct penalty" should be imposed for violations which occur on the playing surface or in the penalty bench area and where the penalized player is readily identifiable.

(a) A misconduct penalty shall be imposed on any player who uses obscene, profane or abusive language to any person or who intentionally knocks or shoots the puck out of the reach of an Official who is retrieving it or who deliberately throws any equipment out of the playing area.

(b) A minor penalty shall be assessed to any player who challenges or disputes the rulings of any Official during a game. If the player persists in such challenge or dispute he shall be assessed a misconduct penalty and any further dispute will result in a game misconduct penalty being assessed to the offending player.

(c) A misconduct penalty shall be imposed on any player or players who bang the boards with their sticks or other instruments any time.

In the event that the Coach, Trainer, Manager or Club Executive commits an infraction under this Rule a bench minor penalty shall be imposed.

(d) A bench minor penalty shall be imposed on the team of any penalized player who does not proceed directly and immediately to the penalty box and take his place on the penalty bench or to the dressing room when so ordered by the Referee.

Where coincident penalties are imposed on players of both teams the penalized players of the visiting team shall take their positions on the penalty bench first in the place designated for visiting players, or where there is no special designation then on the bench farthest from the gate.

(e) Any player who (following a fight or other altercation in which he has been involved is broken up, and for which he is penalized) fails to proceed directly and immediately to the penalty bench; or who causes any delay by retrieving his equipment (gloves, sticks, etc. shall be delivered to him at the penalty bench by his teammates); or who persists in continuing or attempting to continue the fight or altercation; or who resists a Linesman in the discharge of his duties shall incur an automatic fine of one hundred dollars ($100.00) in addition to all other penalties or fines incurred.

(f)   A misconduct penalty shall be imposed on any player who, after warning by the Referee, persists in any course of conduct (including threatening or abusive language or gestures or similar actions) designed to incite an opponent into incurring a penalty.

If, after the assessment of a misconduct penalty a player persists in any course of conduct for which he was previously assessed a misconduct penalty, he shall be assessed a game misconduct penalty.

(g)   In the case of any Club Executive, Manager, Coach or Trainer being guilty of such misconduct, he is to be removed from the bench by order of the Referee, and his case reported to the President for further action.

(h)   If any Club Executive, Manager, Coach or Trainer is removed from the bench by order of the Referee, he must not sit near the bench of his club, nor in any way direct or attempt to direct the play of his club.

(i)   A bench minor penalty shall be imposed against the offending team if any player, any Club Executive, Manager, Coach or Trainer uses obscene, profane or abusive language or gesture to any person or uses the name of any official coupled with any vociferous remarks.

(j)   A bench minor penalty shall be imposed against the offending team if any player, Trainer, Coach, Manager or Club Executive in the vicinity of the players' bench or penalty bench throws anything on the ice during the progress of the game or during stoppage of play.

(NOTE) *The penalty provided under this rule is in addition to any penalty imposed under Rule 46(c) "Broken Stick."*

(k)   A bench minor penalty shall be imposed against the offending team if any player, Trainer, Coach, Manager or Club Executive interferes in any manner with any game official including Referee, Linesmen, Timekeepers or Goal Judges in the performance of their duties.

The Referee may assess further penalties under Rule 67 (Molesting Officials) if he deems them to be warranted.

(l)   A misconduct penalty shall be imposed on any player or players who, except for the purpose of taking their positions on the penalty bench, enter or remain in the Referee's Crease while he is reporting to or consulting with any game

official including Linesmen, Timekeeper, Penalty Timekeeper, Official Scorer or Announcer.

Rule 43.   Adjustment to Clothing and Equipment

(a) Play shall not be stopped, nor the game delayed by reason
     of adjustments to clothing, equipment, shoes, skates or
     sticks.
         For an infringement of this rule, a minor penalty shall be
     given.
(b) The onus of maintaining clothing and equipment in proper
     condition shall be upon the player. If adjustments are
     required, the player shall retire from the ice and play shall
     continue uninterruptedly with a substitute.
(c) No delay shall be permitted for the repair or adjustment of
     goalkeeper's equipment. If adjustments are required, the
     goalkeeper will retire from the ice and his place will be
     taken by the substitute goalkeeper immediately and no
     warm-up will be permitted.
(d) For an infraction of this rule by a goalkeeper, a minor pen-
     alty shall be imposed.

Rule 44.   Attempt to Injure

(a) A match penalty shall be imposed on any player who delib-
     erately attempts to injure an opponent and the circum-
     stances shall be reported to the President for further action.
     A substitute for the penalized player shall be permitted at
     the end of the fifth minute.
(b) A game misconduct penalty shall be imposed on any player
     who deliberately attempts to injure an Official, Manager,
     Coach or Trainer in any manner and the circumstances shall
     be reported to the President for further action.
         (NOTE) *The President, upon preliminary investigation in-
     dicating the probable imposition of supplementary disci-
     plinary action, may order the immediate suspension of a
     player who has incurred a match penalty under this rule,
     pending the final determination of such supplementary disci-
     plinary action.*

Rule 45.   Board-Checking

(a) A minor or major penalty, at the discretion of the Referee
     based upon the degree of violence of the impact with the
     boards, shall be imposed on any player who bodychecks,
     cross-checks, elbows, charges or trips an opponent in such a

manner that causes the opponent to be thrown violently into the boards.

(NOTE) *Any unnecessary contact with a player playing the puck on an obvious "icing" or "off-side" play which results in that player being knocked into the fence is "boarding" and must be penalized as such. In other instances where there is no contact with the fence it should be treated as "charging."*

"Rolling" an opponent (if he is the puck carrier) along the fence where he is endeavouring to go through too small an opening is not boarding. However, if the opponent is not the puck carrier, then such action should be penalized as boarding, charging, interference or if the arms or stick are employed it should be called holding or hooking.

(b) When a major penalty is imposed under this rule for a foul resulting in injury to the face or head of an opponent, an automatic fine of fifty dollars ($50.00) shall be imposed.

Rule 46.   Broken Stick

(a) A player without a stick may participate in the game. A player whose stick is broken may participate in the game provided he drops the broken portion. A minor penalty shall be imposed for an infraction of this rule.

(NOTE) *A broken stick is one which, in the opinion of the Referee, is unfit for normal play.*

(b) A goalkeeper may continue to play with a broken stick until stoppage of play or until he has been legally provided with a stick.

(c) A player whose stick is broken may not receive a stick thrown on to the ice from any part of the rink but must obtain same at his players' bench. A goalkeeper whose stick is broken may not receive a stick thrown on to the ice from any part of the rink but may receive a stick from a teammate without proceeding to his players' bench. A minor penalty plus a misconduct penalty shall be imposed on the player or goalkeeper receiving a stick illegally under this rule.

(d) A goalkeeper whose stick is broken may not go to the players' bench for a replacement but must receive his stick from a teammate.

For an infraction of this rule a minor penalty shall be imposed on the goalkeeper.

Rule 47.   Charging

(a) A minor or major penalty shall be imposed on a player who runs or jumps into or charges an opponent.

(b) When a major penalty is imposed under this rule for a foul, resulting in injury to the face or head of an opponent, an automatic fine of fifty dollars ($50.00) shall be imposed.

(c) A minor or major penalty shall be imposed on a player who charges a goalkeeper while the goalkeeper is within his goal crease.

>   (NOTE) *If more than two steps or strides are taken it shall be considered a charge.*

>   *A goalkeeper is NOT "fair game" just because he is outside the goal crease area. A penalty for interference or charging (minor or major) should be called in every case where an opposing player makes unnecessary contact with a goalkeeper.*

>   *Likewise Referees should be alert to penalize goalkeepers for tripping, slashing or spearing in the vicinity of the goal.*

Rule 48.   Cross-Checking and Butt-Ending

(a) A minor or major penalty, at the discretion of the Referee, shall be imposed on a player who "cross-checks" an opponent.

(b) A major penalty shall be imposed on any player who "butt-ends" or attempts to "butt-end" an opponent.

>   (NOTE) *Attempt to "butt-end" shall include all cases where a "butt-end" gesture is made regardless whether body contact is made or not.*

(c) When a major penalty is imposed under this rule an automatic fine of fifty dollars ($50.00) shall also be imposed.

>   (NOTE) *Cross-check shall mean a check delivered with both hands on the stick and no part of the stick on the ice.*

Rule 49.   Deliberate Injury of Opponents

(a) A match penalty shall be imposed on a player who deliberately injures an opponent in any manner.

>   (NOTE) *Any player wearing tape or any other material on his hands who cuts or injures an opponent during an altercation shall receive a match penalty under this rule.*

(b) In addition to the match penalty, the Referee shall impose a fine of one hundred dollars ($100.00) on any player who deliberately injures another in any manner.

(c) No substitute shall be permitted to take the place of the

penalized player until ten minutes actual playing time shall
have elasped, from the time the penalty was imposed.

(d) A game misconduct penalty shall be imposed on any player
who deliberately injures an Official, Manager, Coach or
Trainer in any manner and the circumstances shall be reported to the President for further action.

(e) A match penalty shall be imposed on any player who deliberately "head-butts" or attempts to "head-butt" an opponent
during an altercation and the circumstances shall be reported to the President for further action. A substitute shall
be permitted at the end of the fifth minute. In the event
there is an injury to an opponent resulting from the foul no
substitute shall be permitted to take the place of the
penalized player until ten minutes actual playing shall be
elapsed.

(NOTE) *The President, upon preliminary investigation indicating the probable imposition of supplementary disciplinary action, may order the immediate suspension of a
player who has incurred a match penalty under this rule,
pending the final determination of such supplementary disciplinary action.*

Rule 50.   **Delaying the Game**

(a) A minor penalty shall be imposed on any player or
goalkeeper who delays the game by deliberately shooting or
batting the puck with his stick outside the playing area.

(NOTE) *This penalty shall apply also when a player or
goalkeeper deliberately bats or shoots the puck with his stick
outside the playing area after a stoppage of play.*

(b) A minor penalty shall be imposed on any player or
goalkeeper who throws or deliberately bats the puck with
his hand or stick outside the playing area.

(c) A minor penalty shall be imposed on any player (including
goalkeeper) who delays the game by deliberately displacing
a goal post from its normal position. The Referee or Linesmen shall stop play immediately when a goal post has been
displaced.

If the goal post is deliberately displaced by a goalkeeper
or player during the course of a "break-away" a penalty
shot will be awarded to the non-offending team, which shot
shall be taken by the player last in possession of the puck.

(NOTE) *A player with a "break-away" is defined as a
player in control of the puck with no opposition between*

*him and the opposing goal and with a reasonable scoring
opportunity.*

If by reason of insufficient time in the regular playing
time or by reason of penalties already imposed the minor
penalty awarded to a player for deliberately displacing his
own goal post cannot be served in its entirety within the regular playing time of the game or at any time in overtime, a
penalty shot shall be awarded against the offending team.

(d) A bench minor penalty shall be imposed upon any team
which, after warning by the Referee to its Captain or Alternate Captain to place the correct number of players on the
ice and commence play, fails to comply with the Referee's
direction and thereby causes any delay by making additional
substitutions, by persisting in having its players off-side, or in
any other manner.

Rule 51.   **Elbowing and Kneeing**
(a) A minor or major penalty, at the discretion of the Referee,
shall be imposed on any player who uses his elbow or knee
in such a manner as to in any way foul an opponent.
(b) When a major penalty is imposed under this rule for a foul
resulting in an injury to an opponent an automatic fine of
fifty dollars ($50.00) shall also be imposed.

Rule 52.   **Face-offs**
(a) The puck shall be "faced-off" by the Referee or the Linesman dropping the puck on the ice between the sticks of the
players "facing-off." Players facing-off will stand squarely
facing their opponents' end of the rink approximately one
stick length apart with the blade of their sticks on the ice.

When the face-off takes place in any of the end face-off
circles the players taking part shall take their positions so
that they will have one skate on each side and clear of the
line running through the face-off spot and with both feet behind and clear of the line parallel to the goal line. The sticks
of both players facing-off shall have the blade on the ice and
entirely clear of the spot or place where the puck is to be
dropped.

No other player shall be allowed to enter the face-off circle or come within fifteen feet of the players facing-off the
puck, and must stand on side on all face-offs.

If a violation of this sub-section of this rule occurs the
Referee or Linesman shall re-face the puck.

(b) If after warning by the Referee or Linesman either of the players fails to take his proper position for the face-off promptly, the Official shall be entitled to face-off the puck notwithstanding such default.

(c) In the conduct of any face-off anywhere on the playing surface no player facing-off shall make any physical contact with his opponent's body by means of his own body or by his stick except in the course of playing the puck after the face-off has been completed.

For violation of this rule the Referee shall impose a minor penalty or penalties on the player(s) whose action(s) caused the physical contact.

(NOTE) *"Conduct of any face-off" commences when the Referee designates the place of the face-off and he (or the Linesman) takes up his position to drop the puck.*

(d) If a player facing-off fails to take his proper position immediately when directed by the Official, the Official may order him replaced for that face-off by any teammate then on the ice.

No substitution of players shall be permitted until the face-off has been completed and play has been resumed.

(e) A second violation of any of the provisions of sub-section (a) hereof by the same team during the same face-off shall be penalized with a minor penalty to the player who commits the second violation of the rule.

(f) When an infringement of a rule has been committed or a stoppage of play has been caused by any player of the attacking side in the Attacking Zone the ensuing face-off shall be made in the Neutral Zone on the nearest face-off spot.

(NOTE) *This includes stoppage of play caused by player of attacking side shooting the puck on to the back of the defending team's net without any intervening action by the defending team.*

(g) When an infringement of a rule has been committed by players of both sides in the play resulting in the stoppage, the ensuing face-off will be made at the place of such infringement or at the place where play is stopped.

(h) When stoppage occurs between the end face-off spots and near end of rink the puck shall be faced-off at the end face-off spot, on the side where the stoppage occurs unless otherwise expressly provided by these rules.

(i) No face-off shall be made within fifteen of the goal or sideboards.

(j) When a goal is illegally scored as a result of a puck being deflected directly from an Official anywhere in the Defending Zone the resulting face-off shall be made at the end face-off spot in the Defending Zone.

(k)   When the game is stopped for any reason not specifically covered in the official rules, the puck must be faced-off where it was last played.

(l)   The whistle will not be blown by the Official to start play. Playing time will commence from the instant the puck is faced-off and will stop when the whistle is blown.

Rule 53.   **Falling on Puck**

(a)   A minor penalty shall be imposed on a player other than the goalkeeper who deliberately falls on or gathers a puck into his body.

(NOTE) *Any player who drops to his knees to block shots should not be penalized if the puck is shot under them or becomes lodged in their clothing or equipment but any use of the hands to make the puck unplayable should be penalized promptly.*

(b)   A minor penalty shall be imposed on a goalkeeper who (when his body is entirely outside the boundaries of his own crease area and when the puck is behind the goal line) deliberately falls on or gathers the puck into his body or who holds or places the puck against any part of the goal or against the boards.

(c)   No defending player, except the goalkeeper, will be permitted to fall on the puck or hold the puck or gather a puck into the body or hands when the puck is within the goal crease.

For infringement of this rule, play shall immediately be stopped and a penalty shot shall be ordered against the offending team, but no other penalty shall be given.

(NOTE) *This rule shall be interpreted so that a penalty shot will be awarded only when the puck is in the crease at the instant the offense occurs. However, in cases where the puck is outside the crease, Rule 53(a) may still apply and a minor penalty may be imposed, even though no penalty shot is awarded.*

Rule 54.   **Fisticuffs**

(a)   A major and a game misconduct penalty or a major penalty, at the discretion of the referee, shall be imposed on any player who starts fisticuffs.

(b)   A minor penalty shall be imposed on a player who, having been struck, shall retaliate with a blow or attempted blow. However, at the discretion of the Referee a major or a double minor penalty may be imposed if such player continues the altercation.

(NOTE 1) *It is the intent and purpose of this rule that the Referee shall impose the "major and game misconduct" penalty in all cases when the instigator of the fight or the retaliator is the aggressor and is plainly doing so for the purpose of intimidation or punishment.*

(NOTE 2) *Referees are directed to employ every means provided by these Rules to stop "brawling" and should use Rule 42(c) for this purpose.*

(c) A misconduct or game misconduct penalty shall be imposed on any player involved in fisticuffs off the playing surface or with another player who is off the playing surface.

(d) A game misconduct penalty shall be imposed on any player or goalkeeper on the ice who is the first to intervene in an altercation then in progress. This penalty is in addition to any other penalty incurred in the same incident.

Rule 55. **Goals and Assists**

(NOTE) *It is the responsibility of the Official Scorer to award goals and assists, and his decision in this respect is final notwithstanding the report of the Referee or any other game official. Such awards shall be made or withheld strictly in accordance with the provisions of this rule. Therefore, it is essential that the Official Scorer shall be thoroughly familiar with every aspect of this rule, be alert to observe all actions which could affect the making of an award and, above all, the awards must be made or withheld with absolute impartiality.*

In case of an obvious error in awarding a goal or an assist which has been announced, it should be corrected promptly but changes should not be made in the official scoring summary after the Referee has signed the Game Report.

(a) A goal shall be scored when the puck shall have been put between the goal posts by the stick of a player of the attacking side, from in front, and below the cross bar, and entirely across a red line, the width of the diameter of the goal posts drawn on the ice from one goal post to the other.

(b) A goal shall be scored if the puck is put into the goal in any way by a player of the defending side. The player of the attacking side who last played the puck shall be credited with the goal but no assist shall be awarded.

(c) If an attacking player kicks the puck and it is deflected into the net by any player of the defending side except the goalkeeper, the goal shall be allowed. The player who kicked the puck shall be credited with the goal but no assist shall be awarded.

(d) If the puck shall have been deflected into the goal from the shot of an attacking player by striking any part of the person of a player of the same side, a goal shall be allowed. The player who deflected the puck shall be credited with the goal. The goal shall not be allowed if the puck has been kicked, thrown or otherwise deliberately directed into the goal by any means other than a stick.

(e) If a goal is scored as a result of a puck being deflected directly into the net from an Official, the goal shall not be allowed.

(f) Should a player legally propel a puck into the goal crease of the opponent club and the puck should become loose and available to another player of the attacking side, a goal scored on the play shall be legal.

(g) Any goal scored, other than as covered by the official rules, shall not be allowed.

(h) A "goal" shall be credited in the scoring records to a player who shall have propelled the puck into the opponents' goal. Each "goal" shall count one point in the player's record.

(i) When a player scores a goal an "assist" shall be credited to the player or players taking part in the play immediately preceding the goal, but not more than two assists can be given on any goal. Each "assist" so credited shall count one point in the player's record.

(j) Only one point can be credited to any one player on a goal.

Rule 56.   **Gross Misconduct**

(a) The Referee may suspend from the game and order to the dressing room for the remainder of the game, any player, Manager, Coach or Trainer guilty of gross misconduct of any kind.

(b) If a player so dismissed is taking part in the game, he shall be charged with a game misconduct penalty, and a substitute shall be permitted.

(c) The Referee in charge is to decide on any violation and report the incident to the President of the League for further action.

Rule 57.   **Handling Puck With Hands**

(a) If a player, except the goalkeeper, closes his hand on the puck the play shall be stopped and a minor penalty shall be imposed on him. A goalkeeper who holds the puck with his hands for longer than three seconds shall be given a minor penalty.

(b) A goalkeeper must not deliberately hold the puck in any manner which in the opinion of the Referee causes a stoppage of play, nor throw the puck forward towards the opponents' goal, nor deliberately drop the puck into his pads or on to the goal net, nor deliberately pile up snow or obstacles at or near his net, that in the opinion of the Referee would tend to prevent the scoring of a goal.

(NOTE) *The object of this entire rule is to keep the puck in play continuously and any action taken by the goalkeeper which causes an unnecessary stoppage must be penalized without warning.*

(c) The penalty for infringement of this rule by the goalkeeper shall be a minor penalty.

(NOTE) *In the case of puck thrown forward by the goalkeeper being taken by an opponent, the Referee shall allow the resulting play to be completed, and if a goal is scored by the non-offending team, it shall be allowed and no penalty given; but if a goal is not scored, play shall be stopped and a minor penalty shall be imposed against the goalkeeper.*

(d) A minor penalty shall be imposed on a player except the goalkeeper who, while play is in progress, picks up the puck off the ice with his hand.

If a player except the goalkeeper, while play is in progress, picks up the puck with his hand from the ice in the goal crease area, the play shall be stopped immediately and a penalty shot shall be awarded to the non-offending team.

(e) A player shall be permitted to stop or "bat" a puck in the air with his open hand, or push it along the ice with his hand, and the play shall not be stopped unless in the opinion of the Referee he has deliberately directed the puck to a teammate, in which case the play shall be stopped and the puck faced-off at the spot where the offense occurred.

(NOTE) *The object of this rule is to ensure continuous action and the Referee should NOT stop play unless he is satisfied that the directing of the puck to a teammate was in fact DELIBERATE.*

The puck may not be "batted" with the hand directly into the net at any time, but a goal shall be allowed when the puck has been legally "batted" or is deflected into the goal by a defending player except the goalkeeper.

Rule 58.   **High Sticks**

(a) The carrying of sticks above the normal height of the shoulder is prohibited, and a minor penalty may be imposed on any player violating this rule, at the discretion of the Referee.

(b) A goal scored from a stick so carried shall not be allowed, except by a player of the defending team.

(c) When a player carries or holds any part of his stick above the height of his shoulder so that injury to the face or head of an opposing player results, the Referee shall have no alternative but to impose a major penalty on the offending player.

When a major penalty is imposed under this rule for a foul resulting in injury to the face or head of an opponent, an automatic fine of fifty dollars ($50.00) shall also be imposed.

(d) Batting the puck above the normal height of the shoulders with the stick is prohibited and when it occurs there shall be a whistle and ensuing face-off at the spot where the offense occurred unless:

1. the puck is batted to an opponent in which case the play shall continue.

2. a player of the defending side shall bat the puck into his own goal in which case the goal shall be allowed.

(NOTE) *When player bats the puck to an opponent under sub-section 1 the Referee shall give the "wash-out" signal immediately. Otherwise he will stop the play.*

(e) When either team is below the numerical strength of its opponent and a player of the team of greater numerical strength causes a stoppage of play by striking the puck with his stick above the height of his shoulder, the resulting face-off shall be made at one of the end face-off spots adjacent to the goal of the team causing the stoppage.

Rule 59.   **Holding an Opponent**

A minor penalty shall be imposed on a player who holds an opponent with hands or stick or in any other way.

Rule 60.   **Hooking**

(a) A minor penalty shall be imposed on a player who impedes or seeks to impede the progress of an opponent by "hooking" with his stick.

(b) A major penalty shall be imposed on any player who injures an opponent by "hooking."

When a major penalty is imposed under this rule for a foul resulting in injury to the face or head of an opponent, an automatic fine of fifty dollars ($50.00) shall also be imposed.

(NOTE) *When a player is checking another in such a way that there is only stick-to-stick contact such action is NOT either hooking or holding.*

Rule 61. Icing the Puck

(a) For the purpose of this rule, the center line will divide the ice into halves. Should any player of a team, equal or superior in numerical strength to the opposing team, shoot, bat or deflect the puck from his own half of the ice, beyond the goal line of the opposing team, play shall be stopped and the puck faced-off at the end face-off of the offending team, unless on the play the puck shall have entered the net of the opposing team, in which case the goal shall be allowed.

For the purpose of this rule the point of last contact with the puck by the team in possession shall be used to determine whether icing has occurred or not.

(NOTE 1) *If during the period of a delayed whistle due to a foul by a player of the side NOT in possession, the side in possession "ices" the puck, then the face-off following the stoppage of play shall take place in the Neutral Zone near the Defending Blue Line of the team "icing" the puck.*

(NOTE 2) *When a team is "short-handed" as the result of a penalty and the penalty is about to expire, the decision as to whether there has been an "icing" shall be determined at the instant the penalty expires, and if the puck crosses the opponents' goal line after the penalty has expired, it is "icing." The action of the penalized player remaining in the penalty box will not alter the ruling.*

(NOTE 3) *For the purpose of interpretation of this rule, "icing the puck" is completed the instant the puck is touched first by a defending player (other than the goalkeeper) after it has crossed the Goal Line and if in the action of so touching the puck, it is knocked or deflected into the net it is NO goal.*

(NOTE 4) *When the puck is shot and rebounds from the body or stick of an opponent in his own half of the ice so as to cross the goal line of the player shooting it shall not be considered as "icing."*

(NOTE 5) *Notwithstanding the provisions of this section concerning "batting" the puck in respect to the "icing the puck" rule, the provisions of the final paragraph of Rule 57(e) apply and NO goal can be scored by batting the puck with the hand into the opponent's goal whether attended or not.*

(NOTE 6) *If while the Linesman has signalled a slow whistle for a clean interception under Rule 71(c), the player intercepting shoots or bats the puck beyond the opponent's goal line in such a manner as to constitute "icing the puck," the Linesman's "slow whistle" shall be considered exhausted the instant the puck crosses the blue line and "icing" shall be called in the usual manner.*

(b) If a player of the side shooting the puck down the ice who is on-side and eligible to play the puck does so before it is touched by an opposing player, the play shall continue and it shall not be considered a violation of this rule.

(c) If the puck was so shot by a player of a side below the numerical strength of the opposing team, play shall continue and the face-off shall not take place.

(d) If, however, the puck shall go beyond the goal line in the opposite half of the ice directly from either of the players while facing-off, it shall not be considered a violation of the rule.

(e) If, in the opinion of the Linesman, a player of the opposing team excepting the goalkeeper is able to play the puck before it passes his goal line, but has not done so, the face-off shall not be allowed and play shall continue. If, in the opinion of the Referee, the defending side intentionally abstains from playing the puck promptly when they are in a position to do so, he shall stop the play and order the resulting face-off on the adjacent corner face-off spot nearest the goal of the team at fault.

(NOTE) *The purpose of this section is to enforce continuous action, and both Referee and Linesmen should interpret and apply the rule to produce this result.*

(f) If the puck shall touch any part of a player of the opposing side or his skates or his stick, or if it passes through any part of the goal crease before it shall have reached his goal line, or shall have touched the goalkeeper or his skates or his stick at any time before or after crossing his goal line, it shall not be considered as "icing the puck" and play shall continue.

(NOTE) *If the goaltender takes any action to dislodge the puck from back of the nets, the icing shall be washed out.*

(g) If the Linesman shall have erred in calling an "icing the puck" infraction (regardless of whether either team is short-handed), the puck shall be faced on the center ice face-off spot.

Rule 62. Interference

(a) A minor penalty shall be imposed on a player who interferes with or impedes the progress of an opponent who is not in possession of the puck, or who deliberately knocks a stick out of an opponent's hand or who prevents a player who has dropped his stick from regaining possession of it or who knocks or shoots any abandoned or broken stick or illegal puck or other debris towards an opposing puck carrier in a manner that could cause him to be distracted. (See also Rule 80(a).)

(NOTE) *The last player to touch the puck—other than a goalkeeper—shall be considered the player in possession. In interpreting this rule the Referee should make sure which of the players is the one creating the interference—often it is the action and movement of the attacking player which causes the interference since the defending players are entitled to "stand their ground" or "shadow" the attacking players. Players of the side in possession shall not be allowed to "run" deliberate interference for the puck carrier.*

(b) A minor penalty shall be imposed on any player on the players' bench or on the penalty bench who by means of his stick or his body interferes with the movements of the puck or of any opponent on the ice during the progress of play.

(c) A minor penalty shall be imposed on a player who, by means of his stick or his body, interferes with or impedes the movements of the goalkeeper by actual physical contact while he is in his goal crease area unless the puck is already in that area.

(d) Unless the puck is in the goal crease area, a player of the attacking side not in possession may not stand on the goal crease line or in the goal crease or hold his stick in the goal crease area, and if the puck should enter the net while such condition prevails, a goal shall not be allowed, and the puck shall be faced in the Neutral Zone at face-off spot nearest the Attacking Zone of the offending team.

(e) If a player of the attacking side has been physically interfered with by the action of any defending player so as to cause him to be in the goal crease, and the puck should enter the net while the player so interfered with is still within the goal crease, the "goal" shall be allowed.

(f) If when the goalkeeper has been removed from the ice any member of his team (including the goalkeeper) not legally on the ice, including the Manager, Coach or Trainer interferes by means of his body or stick or any other object with the movements of the puck or an opposing player, the Referee shall immediately award a goal to the non-offending team.

(g) When a player, in control of the puck in the opponent's side of the center red line, and having no other opponent to pass than the goalkeeper is interfered with by a stick or any part thereof or other object thrown or shot by any member of the defending team including the Manager, Coach, or Trainer, a penalty shot shall be awarded to the non-offending side.

(NOTE) *The attention of Referees is directed particularly to three types of offensive interference which should be penalized;*

(1) *When the defending team secures possession of the puck in its own end and the other players of that team run interference for the puck carrier by forming a protective screen against forechecker;*

(2) *When a player facing-off obstructs his opposite number after the face-off when the opponent is not in possession of the puck;*

(3) *When the puck carrier makes a drop pass and follows through so as to make bodily contact with an opposing player.*

Defensive interference consists of bodily contact with an opposing player who is not in possession of the puck.

Rule 63.   **Interference by Spectators**

(a) In the event of a player being held or interfered with by a spectator, the Referee or Linesman shall blow the whistle and play shall be stopped, unless the team of the player interfered with is in possession of the puck at this time when the play shall be allowed to be completed before blowing the whistle, and the puck shall be faced at the spot where last played at time of stoppage.

(NOTE) *The Referee shall report to the President for disciplinary action, all cases in which a player becomes involved in an altercation with a spectator but no penalty should be imposed.*

(b) Any player who physically interferes with the spectators shall automatically incur a game misconduct penalty and the Referee shall report all such infractions to the President who shall have full power to impose such further penalty as he shall deem appropriate.

(c) In the event that objects are thrown on the ice which interfere with the progress of the game the Referee shall blow the whistle and stop the play, and the puck shall be faced-off at the spot play is stopped.

Rule 64. Kicking Player

A match penalty shall be imposed on any player who kicks or attempts to kick another player.

(NOTE) *Whether or not one injury occurs, the Referee may, at his discretion, impose a ten-minute time penalty under this rule.*

Rule 65. Kicking Puck

Kicking the puck shall be permitted in all zones, but a goal may not be scored by the kick of an attacking player except if an attacking player kicks the puck and it is deflected into the net by any players of the defending side except the goalkeeper.

Rule 66. Leaving Players' Bench or Penalty Bench

(a) No player may leave the players' bench or penalty bench at any time during an altercation. Substitutions made prior to the altercation shall be permitted provided the players so substituting do not enter the altercation.

(b) For violation of this rule a double minor penalty shall be imposed on the player of the team who was first to leave the players' bench or penalty bench during an altercation. If players of both teams leave their respective benches at the same time, the first identifiable player of each team to do so shall incur a double minor penalty. A game misconduct penalty shall also be imposed on any player who is penalized under this sub-section, and the club shall incur a fine of one thousand dollars ($1,000) for the first such incident, three thousand dollars ($3,000) for the second and five thousand dollars ($5,000) for the third and subsequent such incident.

(c) Any player (other than those dealt with under sub-section (b) hereof) who leaves his players' bench during an altercation and is assessed a minor, major or misconduct penalty for his actions, shall also incur an automatic game misconduct penalty.

(d) A player (other than those dealt with under sub-section (b) & (c) hereof) who leaves his players' bench during an altercation, shall be subject to an automatic fine of one hundred dollars ($100.00) and the Referee shall report all such infractions to the President who shall have full power to impose such further penalty as he shall deem appropriate.

(NOTE 1) *This automatic fine shall be imposed in addition to the normal penalties imposed for fouls committed by the player after he has left the players' bench.*

(NOTE 2) *For the purpose of determining which player was first to leave his players' bench during an altercation the Referee may consult with the Linesmen or Minor Officials.*

(e) In regular League games, any player who incurs a *second* penalty under sub-section (b) hereof (for leaving the players' bench first) shall be suspended automatically for the next League game of his team. For each subsequent violation, the automatic suspension shall be increased by one game.

In play-off games, any player, who incurs a penalty under sub-section (b) hereof (for leaving the players' bench first), shall be suspended automatically for the next play-off game of his team. For each subsequent violation, this automatic suspension shall be increased by one game.

The automatic suspensions incurred under this sub-section in respect to League games shall have no effect with respect to violations during play-off games.

(f) Except at the end of each period, or on expiration of penalty, no player may at any time leave the penalty bench.

(g) A penalized player who leaves the penalty bench before his penalty has expired, whether play is in progress or not, shall incur an additional minor penalty, after serving his unexpired penalty.

(h) Any penalized player leaving the penalty bench during stoppage of play and during an altercation shall incur a minor penalty plus a game misconduct penalty after serving his unexpired time.

(i) If a player leaves the penalty bench before his penalty is fully served, the Penalty Timekeeper shall note the time and signal the Referee who will immediately stop play.

(j) In the case of a player returning to the ice before his time has expired through an error of the Penalty Timekeeper, he is not to serve an additional penalty, but must serve his unexpired time.

(k) If a player of an attacking side in possession of the puck shall be in such a position as to have no opposition between him and the opposing goalkeeper, and while in such position he shall be interfered with by a player of the opposing side who shall have illegally entered the game, the Referee shall impose a penalty shot against the side to which the offending player belongs.

(l) If the opposing goalkeeper has been removed and an attacking player in possession of the puck shall have no player of the defending team to pass and a stick or a part thereof or any other object is thrown or shot by an opposing player or the player is fouled from behind thereby being prevented from having a clear shot on an open goal, a goal shall be awarded against the offending team.

  If when the opposing goalkeeper has been removed from the ice a player of the side attacking the unattended goal is interfered with by a player who shall have entered the game illegally, the Referee shall immediately award a goal to the non-offending team.

(m) If a Coach or Manager gets on the ice after the start of a period and before that period is ended, the Referee shall impose a bench minor penalty against the team and report the incident to the President for disciplinary action.

(n) Any Club Executive or Manager committing the same offense, will be automatically fined two hundred dollars ($200.00).

(o) If a penalized player returns to the ice from the penalty bench before his penalty has expired by his own error or the error of the Penalty Timekeeper, any goal scored by his own team while he is illegally on the ice shall be disallowed, but all penalties imposed on either team shall be served as regular penalties.

(p) If a player shall illegally enter the game from his own players' bench or from the penalty bench, any goal scored by his own team while he is illegally on the ice shall be disallowed, but all penalties imposed against either team shall be served as regular penalties.

Rule 67.   **Molesting Officials**

(a) Any player who touches or holds a Referee, Linesman or any game Official with his hand or his stick or trips or body-checks any of such officials, shall receive a ten-minute misconduct penalty or a game misconduct penalty. The use of a substitute for the player so suspended shall be permitted.

(b) Any Club Executive, Manager, Coach or Trainer who holds or strikes an Official, shall be automatically suspended from the game, ordered to the dressing room, and a substantial fine shall be imposed by the President.

Rule 68.   **Obscene or Profane Language or Gestures**

(a) Players shall not use obscene gestures on the ice or any-where in the rink before, during or after the game. For a vi-olation of this rule a game misconduct penalty shall be im-posed and the Referee shall report the circumstances to the President of the League for further disciplinary action.

(b) Players shall not use profane language on the ice or any-where in the rink before, during or after a game. For viola-tion of this rule, a misconduct penalty shall be imposed ex-cept when the violation occurs in the vicinity of the players bench in which case a bench minor penalty shall be im-posed.

(NOTE) *It is the responsibility of all game Officials and all Club Officials to send a confidential report to the President setting out the full details concerning the use of obscene ges-tures or language by any player, Coach or other Official. The President shall take such further disciplinary action as he shall deem appropriate.*

(c) Club Executives, Managers, Coaches, and Trainers shall not use obscene or profane language or gestures anywhere in the rink. For violation of this rule a bench minor penalty shall be imposed.

Rule 69.   **Off-Sides**

(a) The position of the player's skates and not that of his stick shall be the determining factor in all instances in deciding an "off-side." A player is off-side when both skates are com-pletely over the outer edge of the determining center line or blue line involved in the play.

(NOTE 1) *A player is "on-side" when "either" of his skates are in contact with or on his own side of the line at the instant the puck completely crosses the outer edge of that line regardless of the position of his stick.*

(NOTE 2) *It should be noted that while the position of the player's skates is what determines whether a player is "off-side," nevertheless the question of "off-side" never arises until the puck has completely crossed the outer edge of the line at which time the decision is to be made.*

(b) If in the opinion of the Linesman an intentional off-side play has been made, the puck shall be faced-off at the end face-off spot in the Defending Zone of the offending team.

(NOTE 3) *This rule does not apply to a team below the numerical strength of its opponent. In such cases the puck shall be faced-off at the spot from which the pass was made.*

(NOTE 4) *An intentional off-side is one which is made for the purpose of securing a stoppage of play regardless of the reason, or where an off-side play is made under conditions where there is no possibility of completing a legal pass.*

(c) If the Linesmen shall have erred in calling an off-side pass infraction (regardless of whether either team is short-handed) the puck shall be faced on the center ice face-off spot.

Rule 70. Passes

(a) The puck may be passed by any player to a player of the same side within any one of the three zones into which the ice is divided, but may not be passed forward from a player in one zone to a player of the same side in another zone, except by a player on the defending team, who may make and take forward passes from their own Defending Zone to the center line without incurring an off-side penalty. This "forward pass" from the Defending Zone must be completed by the pass receiver who is legally on-side at the center line.

(NOTE 1) *The position of the puck (not the player's skates) shall be determining factor in deciding from which zone the pass was made.*

(NOTE 2) *Passes may be completed legally at the center red line in exactly the same manner as passes at the attacking blue line.*

(b) Should the puck, having been passed, contact any part of the body, stick or skates of a player of the same side who is legally on-side, the pass shall be considered to have been completed.

(c) The player last touched by the puck shall be deemed to be in possession.

Rebounds off goalkeeper's pads or other equipment shall

not be considered as a change of possession or the completion of the play by the team when applying Rule 34(b).

(d) If a player in the Neutral Zone is preceded into the Attacking Zone by the puck passed from the Neutral Zone, he shall be eligible to take possession of the puck anywhere in the Attacking Zone except when the "icing the puck" rule applies.

(e) If a player in the same zone from which a pass is made is preceded by the puck into succeeding zones, he shall be eligible to take possession of the puck in that zone except where the "icing the puck" rule applies.

(f) If an attacking player passes the puck backward toward his own goal from the Attacking Zone, an opponent may play the puck anywhere regardless of whether he (the opponent) was in the same zone at the time the puck was passed or not. (*No "slow whistle."*)

Rule 71.   Preceding Puck into Attacking Zone

(a) Players of an attacking team must not precede the puck into the Attacking Zone.

(b) For violation of this rule, the play is stopped, and puck shall be faced-off in the Neutral Zone at face-off spot nearest the Attacking Zone of the offending team.

   (NOTE) *A player actually propelling the puck who shall cross the line ahead of the puck, shall not be considered "off-side."*

(c) If however, notwithstanding the fact that a member of the attacking team shall have preceded the puck into the Attacking Zone, the puck be cleanly intercepted by a member of the defending team at or near the blue line, and be carried or passed by them into the Neutral Zone, the "off-side" shall be ignored and play permitted to continue.

   (*Officials will carry out this rule by means of the "slow whistle."*)

(d) If a player legally carries or passes the puck back into his own Defending Zone while a player of the opposing team is in such Defending Zone, the "off-side" shall be ignored and play permitted to continue.

   (*No "slow whistle."*)

Rule 72.   Puck Out of Bounds or Unplayable

(a) When the puck goes outside the playing area at either end, or either side of the rink or strikes any obstacles above the playing surface other than the boards, glass or wire, it shall be faced-off from whence it was shot or deflected, unless otherwise expressly provided in these rules.

(b)   When the puck becomes lodged in the netting on the outside of either goal so as to make it unplayable, or if it is frozen between opposing players intentionally or otherwise, the Referee shall stop the play and face-off the puck at either of the adjacent face-off spots unless, in the opinion of the Referee, the stoppage was caused by a player of the attacking team, in which case the resulting face-off shall be conducted in the Neutral Zone.

(NOTE) *This includes stoppage of play caused by player of attacking side shooting the puck on to the back of the defending team's net without any intervening action by the defending team.*

The defending team and/or the attacking team may play the puck off the net at any time. However, should the puck remain on the net for longer than three seconds, play shall be stopped and the face-off shall take place in the end face-off zone except when the stoppage is caused by the attacking team, then the face-off shall take place on a face-off spot in the Neutral Zone.

(c)   A minor penalty shall be imposed on a goalkeeper who deliberately drops the puck on the goal netting to cause a stoppage of play.

(d)   If the puck comes to rest on top of the boards surrounding the playing area, it shall be considered to be in play and may be played legally by hand or stick.

Rule 73.   **Puck Must Be Kept in Motion**
(a)   The puck must at all times be kept in motion.
(b)   Except to carry the puck behind its goal once, a side in possession of the puck in its own defense area shall always advance the puck towards the opposing goal, except if it shall be prevented from so doing by players of the opposing side.

For the first infraction of this rule play shall be stopped and a face-off shall be made at either end face-off spot adjacent to the goal of the team causing the stoppage, and the Referee shall warn the Captain or Alternate Captain of the offending team of the reason for the face-off. For a second violation by any player of the same team in the same period a minor penalty shall be imposed on the player violating the rule.

(c)   A minor penalty shall be imposed on any player including the goalkeeper who holds, freezes or plays the puck with his stick, skates or body along the boards in such a manner as to cause a stoppage of play unless he is actually being checked by an opponent.

(d) A player beyond his defense area shall not pass nor carry the puck backward into his Defense Zone for the purpose of delaying the game except when his team is below the numerical strength of the opponents on the ice.

(e) For an infringement of this rule, the face-off shall be at the nearest end face-off spot in the Defending Zone of the offending team.

Rule 74.   Puck Out of Sight and Illegal Puck

(a) Should a scramble take place, or a player accidentally fall on the puck, and the puck be out of sight of the Referee, he shall immediately blow his whistle and stop the play. The puck shall then be "faced-off" at the point where the play was stopped, unless otherwise provided for in the rules.

(b) If at any time while play is in progress a puck other than the one legally in play shall appear on the playing surface, the play shall not be stopped but shall continue with the legal puck until the play then in progress is completed by change of possession.

Rule 75.   Puck Striking Official

Play shall not be stopped if the puck touches an Official anywhere on the rink, regardless of whether a team is short-handed or not.

Rule 76.   Refusing to Start Play

(a) If, when both teams are on the ice, one team for any reason shall refuse to play when ordered to do so by the Referee, he shall warn the Captain or Alternate Captain and allow the team so refusing fifteen seconds within which to begin the game or resume play. If at the end of that time the team shall still refuse to play, the Referee shall impose a two-minute penalty on a player of the offending team to be designated by the Manager or Coach of that team, through the playing Captain; and should there be a repetition of the same incident the Referee shall notify the Manager or Coach that he has been fined the sum of two hundred dollars ($200.00), and should there be a recurrence of the same incident, the Referee shall have no alternative but to declare that the game be forfeited to the non-offending club, and the case shall be reported to the President for further action.

(b) If a team, when ordered to do so by the Referee, through its Club Executive, Manager or Coach, fails to go on the ice and start play within five minutes, the Club Executive, Manager or Coach shall be fined five hundred dollars ($500.00); the game shall be forfeited, and the case shall be reported to the President for further action.

(NOTE) *The President of the League shall issue instructions pertaining to records, etc., of a forfeited game.*

Rule 77.   Slashing

(a) A minor or major penalty, at the discretion of the Referee, shall be imposed on any player who impedes or seeks to impede the progress of an opponent by "slashing" with his stick.

(b) A major penalty shall be imposed on any player who injures an opponent by slashing. When a major penalty is imposed under this rule for a foul resulting in injury to the face or head of an opponent, an automatic fine of fifty dollars ($50.00) shall also be imposed.

(NOTE) *Referees should penalize as "slashing" any player who swings his stick at any opposing player (whether in or out of range) without actually striking him or where a player on the pretext of playing the puck makes a wild swing at the puck with the object of intimidating an opponent.*

(c) Any player who swings his stick at another player in the course of any altercation shall be subject to a fine of not less than two hundred dollars ($200.00), with or without suspension, to be imposed by the President.

(NOTE) *The Referee shall impose the normal appropriate penalty provided in the other sections of this rule and shall in addition report promptly to the President all infractions under this section.*

Rule 78.   Spearing

(a) A major penalty shall be imposed on a player who spears or attempts to spear an opponent.

(NOTE) *"Attempt to spear" shall include all cases where a spearing gesture is made regardless of whether bodily contact is made or not.*

(b) In addition to the major penalty imposed under this rule an automatic fine of $50.00 will also be imposed.

(NOTE 1) *"Spearing" shall mean stabbing an opponent with the point of the stick blade while the stick is being carried with one hand or both hands.*

(NOTE 2) *Spearing may also be treated as a "deliberate attempt to injure" under Rule 44.*

Rule 79.   **Start of Game and Periods**

(a) The game shall be commenced at the time scheduled by a "face-off" in the center of the rink and shall be renewed promptly at the conclusion of each intermission in the same manner.

No delay shall be permitted by reason of any ceremony, exhibition, demonstration or presentation unless consented to reasonably in advance by the visiting team.

(b) Home clubs shall have the choice of goals to defend at the start of the game except where both players' benches are on the same side of the rink, in which case the home club shall start the game defending the goal nearest to its own bench. The teams shall change ends for each succeeding regular or overtime period.

(c) During the pre-game warm-up (which shall not exceed twenty minutes in duration) and before the commencement of play in any period each team shall confine its activity to its own end of the rink so as to leave clear an area thirty feet wide across the center of the Neutral Zone.

(NOTE 1) *The Game Timekeeper shall be responsible for signalling the commencement and termination of the pre-game warm-up and any violation of this rule by the players shall be reported to the President by the Supervisor when in attendance at game.*

(NOTE 2) *Players shall not be permitted to come on the ice during a stoppage in play or at the end of the first and second periods for the purpose of warming-up. The Referee will report any violation of this rule to the President for disciplinary action.*

(d) Fifteen minutes before the time scheduled for the start of the game both teams shall vacate the ice and proceed to their dressing rooms while the ice is being flooded. Both teams shall be signalled by the Game Timekeeper to return to the ice together in time for the scheduled start of the game.

(e) When a team fails to appear on the ice promptly without proper justification a fine shall be assessed against the offending team. The amount of the fine to be decided by the President.

Rule 80.   **Throwing Stick**

(a) When any player of the defending side, including the goalkeeper or Manager, Coach or Trainer, deliberately throws or shoots his stick or any part thereof or any other object, at the puck in his Defending Zone, the Referee shall allow the play to be completed and if a goal is not scored a penalty shot shall be awarded to the non-offending side, which shot shall be taken by the player designated by the Referee as the player fouled.

If, however, the goal being unattended and the attacking player having no defending player to pass and having a chance to score on an "open net," a stick or part thereof or any other object, be thrown by a defending player thereby preventing a shot on the "open net" a goal shall be awarded to the attacking side.

(NOTE 1) *If the officials are unable to determine the person against whom the offense was made the offended team through the Captain shall designate the player on the ice at the time the offense was committed who will take the shot.*

(NOTE 2) *For the purpose of this rule, an open net is defined as one from which a goaltender has been removed for an additional attacking player.*

(b) A major penalty shall be imposed on any player *on the ice* who throws his stick or any part thereof or any other object in the direction of the puck carrier in any zone, except when such act has been penalized by the assessment of a penalty shot or the award of a goal.

(NOTE) *When a player discards the broken portion of a stick by tossing it to the side of the ice (and not over the boards) in such a way as will not interfere with play or opposing player, no penalty will be imposed for so doing.*

(c) The Referee and Linesmen shall report promptly to the President for disciplinary action in every case where a stick or any part thereof is thrown outside the playing area.

Rule 81.   **Time of Match**

(a) The time allowed for a game shall be three twenty-minute periods of actual play with a rest intermission between periods.

Play shall be resumed promptly following each intermission upon the expiry of fifteen minutes from the completion

of play in the preceding period. A preliminary warning shall
be given by the Game Timekeeper to the officials and to
both teams three minutes prior to the resumption of play in
each period, and the final warning shall be given in sufficient
time to enable the teams to resume play promptly.

(NOTE) *For the purpose of keeping the spectators informed as to the time remaining during intermissions, the
Game Timekeeper will use the electric clock to record
length of intermissions.*

(b) The team scoring the greatest number of goals during the
three twenty-minute periods shall be the winner, and shall
be credited with two points in the League standing.

(c) In the intervals between periods, the ice surface shall be
flooded unless mutually agreed to the contrary.

(d) If any unusual delay occurs within five minutes of the end
of the first or second periods, the Referee may order the
next regular intermission to be taken immediately and the
balance of the period will be completed on the resumption
of play with the teams defending the same goals, after
which the teams will change ends and resume play of the
ensuing period without delay.

(NOTE) *If a delay takes place with more than five minutes
remaining in the first or second period, the Referee will
order the next regular intermission to be taken immediately
only when requested to do so by the Home Club.*

Rule 82.   **Tied Games**

(a) If, at the end of the three regular twenty-minute periods, the
score shall be tied, the game shall be called a "TIE," and
each team shall be credited with one point in the League
standing.

(b) Special conditions for duration and number of periods of
play-off games, shall be arranged by the Board of Gover-
nors.

Rule 83.   **Tripping**

(a) A minor penalty shall be imposed on any player who shall
place his stick, knee, foot, arm, hand or elbow in such a
manner that it shall cause his opponent to trip or fall.

(NOTE) *If in the opinion of the Referee a player is unquestionably hook-checking the puck and obtains possession of it,
thereby tripping the puck carrier, no penalty shall be imposed.*

(b) When a player in control of the puck in the opponent's side of the center red line, and having no other opponent to pass than the goalkeeper, is tripped or otherwise fouled from behind thus preventing a reasonable scoring opportunity, a penalty shot shall be awarded to the non-offending side. Nevertheless the Referee shall not stop the play until the attacking side has lost possession of the puck to the defending side.

(NOTE 1) *The intention of this rule is to restore a reasonable scoring opportunity which has been lost by reason of a foul from behind when the foul is committed in the opponent's side of the center red line.*

By "control of the puck" is meant the act of propelling the puck with the stick. If while it is being propelled the puck is touched by another player or his equipment or hits the goal or goes free, the player shall no longer be considered to be "in control of the puck."

(NOTE 2) *Accidental trips occurring simultaneously with or after stoppage of play will not be penalized.*

(c) If, when the opposing goalkeeper has been removed from the ice, a player in control of the puck is tripped or otherwise fouled with no opposition between him and the opposing goal, thus preventing a reasonable scoring opportunity, the Referee shall immediately stop the play and award a goal to the attacking team.

Rule 84.　　　　　　　　**Unnecessary Roughness**

At the discretion of the Referee, a minor penalty may be imposed on any player deemed guilty of unnecessary roughness.

About the Author

One of the few officials inducted into the Hockey Hall of Fame, Bill Chadwick was an outstanding National Hockey League referee for fourteen seasons. It was Chadwick who pioneered the use of the official hand signals common to all hockey today. A student of the rules, he is respected as one who has always called 'em as he sees 'em, a characteristic manifest in the radio and television broadcasting that he has done for years for the New York Rangers. Chadwick is known as "The Big Whistle," the title of his autobiography, written with Hal Bock.